# HOMER

*A Tornado Wrapped
in
Barbed Wire*

by
SCOTT EUBANKS

Copyright © 2021 Stephen F. Austin State University Press

Printed in the United States
All rights reserved.
First Edition

IBSN: 978-1-62288-407-0

*This book is dedicated to all of the undeclared heroes who have walked among the masses for thousands of years. They are the people who have used a bit of their time on Earth to share their wisdom, bravery, and goodness with others with whom their lives have crossed paths. They have become models for others to imitate, and they are the cornerstones of the foundation on which others have built their character.*

*If we are lucky, we have had at least one hero in our life. If we are even luckier, we have been a hero to someone else. If you have a secret hero, tell them what they have meant to you and thank them.*

# CONTENTS

Introduction/Author's Note . . . . *7*

Marshall, Texas, March 4-5, 1963 . . . . *9*
Hamilton, Texas, October 10, 1908 . . . . *12*
Pickin' Cotton . . . . *16*
Storm Clouds over Hamilton . . . . *21*
Peno Bottom, Oklahoma, 1920 . . . . *26*
Homer's First Kiss and Near Drowning . . . . *31*
Going to Town with Papa . . . . *37*
Papa Takes a Wife . . . . *40*
Birthday in a Box . . . . *44*
The Eubanks Kids Spread Out . . . . *54*
The Courtship of Zelma Chance . . . . *66*
Three Marks on a Milk Bottle . . . . *69*
The Wrong Homer Eubanks . . . . *72*
Homer and Zee Sink Their Roots . . . . *77*
Open for Business . . . . *84*
Homer's Wartime Dilemma . . . . *89*
Adjusting to Post-War America . . . . *98*
A Man of Axtion . . . . *103*
Homer's Modus Operandi . . . . *109*
Homer Doses His Boys with Optimism . . . . *117*
Homer the Teacher . . . . *121*
Homer's Rules . . . . *126*
Pig's Feet, High Noon, and Alley Cat . . . . *131*
The Paradox He Was . . . . *137*
Homer's End Times . . . . *141*
Marshall, Texas, March 7, 1963 . . . . *146*
Epilogue . . . . *149*

## Introduction/Author's Note

This book is about an unsung hero and the hardships Homer and too many others faced during the first half of the 20th-Century: poverty, World War I, the Spanish Flu that killed more than fifty million people worldwide, the Dust Bowl, the Great Depression, and World War II. He obviously was not the only person of that time in America deserving of the hero label; he was just the one I knew best. It was a time that ran over the weak and produced a generation of strong, tough, battle-scarred folks that dealt with more adversity than anyone deserved in one lifetime.

The subject of this biography is Homer Eubanks. He was born in 1908 in Hamilton, Texas, and he died in 1963 in Tyler, Texas. He was a sharecropper's son. His journey through life was a trip on a very rocky road. He started it with no money, an eighth-grade education, eight siblings that loved him, and an inner strength that served him well in the face of huge challenges and moments of danger.

I consider this story a historical biography. It is a story about Homer, to be sure. However, it is also a story of a time in American history that too often left one alone to deal with the heartless obstacles that stood between him and a better life. It was a time when families pooled their meager assets, blood, sweat, and tears to help each other cope with economic stress and other angry circumstances that fought to hold them in the darkness as they strained to reach the light. People relied on the kindness and help of others as they clawed their ways in the direction of respectability and a modicum of success. Homer had the help of others, but it was his raw-boned, fierce effort that primarily got him into the greener pastures of life.

**Scott Eubanks**
**Author**

## Marshall, Texas
## March 4-5, 1963

When I got home from high school baseball practice late on the afternoon of Monday, March 4th, 1963, in Marshall, Texas, I was hot, tired, and sweaty, and I headed straight for the refrigerator in search of something cold to drink. With a large glass of iced tea in my hand, I made my way to the television. My plan was to turn it on and zip through the three channels we could get in those pre-cable days in search of something interesting to watch while I cooled down. While waiting for the horizontal bars to clear from the screen of our old Zenith, I noticed a bottle of Old Spice cologne sitting on top of the tv accompanied by a short note from my dad that read, "Scottie (he always misspelled "Scotty"), you can use this cologne while I'm gone." He signed it with three vertical marks underscored by three horizontal marks. The three marks meant "I love you." The story behind the three marks is told in greater detail later in this book, but the signing of all family correspondence with the three "I love you" marks had started when Daddy began putting them on all his notes to mother while they were dating.

I was glad to have the Old Spice. However, it was the note and the three marks that held my attention. I stared at the three marks and was truly warmed by Dad's expression of love for me. It was easier for him to tell me and my two older brothers he loved us this way than it was for him to say it out loud, although he occasionally did. I knew the note meant Dad had already left for a week-long business trip to Tyler, a small city about an hour's drive west of Marshall. I was a little sorry I had not made it home in time to see Dad off, but he spent most weeks on the road, so I was used to seeing him mostly just on weekends. He would be home Friday afternoon.

My father, Homer Eubanks, died Tuesday morning, March 5th, 1963, at Mother Frances Hospital in Tyler, Texas from an unexpected heart attack. He was 54. He would not be coming home Friday.

My oldest brother, Homer, Jr., worked with our dad and was in Tyler with him at the time of his death. In fact, he drove Dad to the hospital where he died within one hour of their arrival. Homer, Jr. called us from the hospital and told Mother and me to get to Tyler as soon as possible. I was getting ready to go to school and Mother was dressing for her beauty shop appointment. Tuesdays were her days off and an appointment with Daisy Power at her shop above Stacy's Shoe Repair on Tuesdays was a longstanding tradition. He also had me call our brother, Robert, who lived in New Orleans, with the news. Robert caught a plane to Shreveport within the hour. Homer, Jr. told me Dad would probably die before we could make the 55-mile trip to Tyler, a message I relayed to Robert. We picked up Homer, Jr.'s wife, Freddie, and made a mad dash to Tyler. Once at the hospital, we sprinted to the emergency room where my brother met us with devastating news: Daddy had passed away within the last 20 minutes. It was the first time I came to the realization that heroes truly were mortal.

The cardiologist, Dr. Richard Hurst, tried valiantly to keep Dad's heart beating, but to no avail. He was kind and gentle with us and took us into the room where Dad's body still lay on the hospital bed. Mother wept uncontrollably and talked to Daddy as though he were still alive. She kept her cheek next to his still warm cheek, and, after Homer and I gave Daddy a farewell kiss on his other cheek, my big brother and I stepped into the hallway to allow Mother a chance to say her goodbye to Daddy in private.

Even in death, hospitals have an insatiable appetite for paperwork and sometimes, a nasty attitude until the grieving clients have completed it. When Mother and Homer, Jr. finished the red tape, we headed for Dad's motel room to retrieve his belongings. Once in his room, we went about our business quietly and thoughtfully.

Each piece of Daddy's belongings we picked up to re-pack caused us to reflect on his former use of it. We performed our task in a trance; a trance that was occasionally broken by sobs, head-shakes, and pauses for wiping away tears. I sat on the edge of Daddy's bed to rest from the massive weight his death had left on my arms, shoulders, and legs. It was as if death didn't just come and go, but, instead, lingered and physically hurt those who mourned the loss of a loved one.

Once Daddy's and Homer Jr.'s's gear was loaded, our three car caravan eased out of the motel parking lot and headed back to Marshall. Homer drove his car and had Mother as a passenger. Freddie drove Mother's car and I drove Daddy's 1963 Ford Galaxy.

I had driven Dad's car many times but for obvious reasons, this time was very different. I was never aware of his smell before, until now. It was a surprisingly pleasant mixture of Camel cigarettes, his Lilac Vegetal aftershave, and starch from his white shirts. I had never noticed before how he kept two or three toothpicks stuck up on his sun visor.

I turned on his radio and punched the buttons that moved the dial to pre-selected stations. They were set to the stations I had selected when we first got the car. Knowing Daddy had spent countless hours in this car, I purposely took a detailed visual and mental inventory of its interior, straining to soak-up his presence as best I could. My tears bore witness to my reluctance to give him up.

Driving Dad's car back to Marshall was gut-wrenching, emotionally weighty, and somewhat cathartic. I needed this time to be alone with Daddy within the confines of his car. I was sixteen years old and did not know how to handle his death. It gave me uninterrupted time to reflect on Daddy's life. He had lived an often rocky, challenge-filled life that certainly had its victories and happy times to balance out the hard times. I was grateful for the time to assess the massive influence he had on my brothers and me. I was grateful I had listened so intently to Daddy when he regaled us boys with stories of his life. He was a great storyteller and a wonderful teacher to his three sons. We, in turn, became great listeners when he spoke.

Homer Eubanks was the seventh of nine children born to sharecroppers in Hamilton, Texas, a small town west of Waco. He was a fighter and a tough man. He valued family and the strength a good family could marshal when all its members worked in unison. He met life and the many bad hands it dealt him head on. He didn't win all of his conflicts, but he never lost his optimism or faith in himself and God. He didn't die wealthy or famous, but his story, which was so rich in content, is worth telling.

**Here's Homer's story.**

## Hamilton, Texas
## October 10, 1908

Polly Eubanks had been awake since 4 a.m., but she lay as still as she could so Robert, her husband of 14 years, could get a couple more hours of sleep before starting another day in the cotton fields shortly after dawn. The picking season had just begun, and his work was hard. He needed his rest. She bit down on her bottom lip rather than cry out from the sharp pains that were attacking her enlarged belly with increasing regularity. Having already given birth to six children, Polly was no stranger to labor pains. She knew number seven was getting very close to joining the family so, a few minutes before sunrise, she shook Robert awake and gave him little time to clear the cobwebs from his sleep-soaked brain before prodding him into action.

Polly quickly took charge of the emerging situation and told Robert, "Wake Aubrey up and send him to fetch Josey and tell her there's no time to waste." Josey was Josephine Jordan, Polly's friend and the best midwife in Hamilton County, Texas. She then told him to rouse Vina up and have her start boiling plenty of water and bring the torn rags she had stored in the cupboard to the bedroom. Polly wasn't making requests, she was issuing orders, and Robert, or Papa, as he was called by his family, knew there'd be hell to pay if he drug his feet.

The smallish white clapboard farmhouse, which sat on 160 acres three miles west of Hamilton, Texas, in the Leesville Community, sprang to life, as though the arrival of child number seven was an event for which the entire family had rehearsed.

Thirteen-year-old Vina was the oldest of the Eubanks children and leadership came easy for her. She rode herd on all of her siblings like a trail boss did his cattle. She inelegantly punctuated her orders to her siblings with brimstone and cuss words that put the fear of God in each of them. She was the oldest child, an effective cusser, and headstrong, totally ignoring her mama's pleas to quit cussing. Papa once washed her mouth out with lye soap. When the cleansing was over, Vina looked straight at her Papa and said, "Well that didn't change a damn thing. May I now get back to my chores?" None of the kids ever dared to challenge Vina's authority, so when she told her nine-year-old brother Alfred–known as "Ab"– to stoke the fire, light the lamps, and hang a lantern on the front porch, he did it. No complaints; he just did it. Six-year-old Bonnie was dispatched to the kitchen to make biscuits and gravy for the family and to boil a pot of strong coffee for Papa and the soon-to-arrive Mrs. Jordan, who would help Mama through the delivery. Of course, Vina would be at her side to supervise.

Aub, who had just turned 11 the week before, rode the family's small pinto pony, Dan, to the Jordan's farm a mile and a quarter down a well-traveled dirt road. When he woke up the Jordans with his call for midwifery, Mr. Jordan hitched his horse up to his buggy. Aub tied Dan to the rear of the buggy, took the reins, and drove himself and Mrs. Jordan back to where his mama waited. This routine had played out before, as Mrs. Jordan had assisted in the births of two of Aub's younger brothers, A.T., aged four, and Paul, now two. In turn, Polly had been on hand when Sarah Jordan had been born in 1904.

Bon had finished her kitchen chores and took A.T. and Paul outside to make certain they stayed out of everyone's way. Aub and Ab sat on the front porch. They were out of the way, but close enough to hear what was going on inside and near enough to respond if they were called upon for more firewood or well water. Vina? She ignored Mrs. Jordan's suggestion to leave the bedroom and stayed bedside holding her mama's hand and dabbing her perspiring brow throughout the ordeal of childbirth. Papa disappeared into the barn after leaving word with Aub to let him know when his new son or daughter arrived. Papa felt pretty certain the new baby would be a boy. He based his supposition on the fact that Polly had carried the baby low and to the right. He knew that when a cow carried its calf that way, it was usually a male. He was torn between hanging around the house until after the birth and going cotton pickin' in the harvest-ready fields. He did neither, opting instead to busy himself by tidying up the barn.

Mrs. Jordan arrived with a carpetbag full of items she thought she might need in delivering the baby. She unloaded a bottle of castor oil, a bottle of primrose oil, scissors, a well-honed butcher knife and lots of rags. When she assessed Polly's situation, she decided natural birth was imminent, so neither the castor oil nor the primrose oil would be needed to induce labor.

When the boys on the porch and Bon, A.T., and Paul, who were in the backyard, heard their mama let out a scream, they all knew their new sibling was about to appear. Well, they all knew except for A.T. and Paul, who were busy running and playing. They seemed oblivious to the scream of pain from their mama. Within minutes of the final scream, Vina ran out on the porch and told Aub to go to the barn and tell Papa he had a new son and that Mama and baby were fine.

Homer Alvin was born at 10:45 a.m., Friday, October 10, 1908. His mother, an avid reader of the classics, had recently finished Homer's *Iliad*, prompting her to name her new son after the great Greek poet. With his first breath, Homer had unknowingly started down the rocky road of life, one destined to be filled with rough edges, tough financial times, soul-hungry demons, physical challenges, and struggles for balance in his manhood. Troubles? You bet, but, also, a life overflowing with love and fun.

Papa's first look at his new son was in the kitchen when Mrs. Jordan laid the newborn in the food scale for his first weigh-in. The red-faced, sandy-haired little fellow tipped the scales at 10 pounds, 3 ounces. All of the other kids had also gathered in the kitchen for the weighing. They then timidly traipsed behind their smiling, proud Papa as he went into the bedroom to check on his Polly. Even though she looked tired and spent, Polly greeted her family with a loving smile that let everyone know all was fine.

Papa always thought his wife looked her prettiest right after giving birth.

After satisfying himself that Polly was okay and that Vina and Bon could manage things for the rest of the day, Papa, Aub, and Ab headed for the cotton fields to pick as many rows as they could before sunset. The celebration was over. It was time for the Eubanks Family to continue its struggle for survival as sharecroppers.

## Pickin' Cotton

Pickin' cotton was hard work. It required the picker to bend at the waist and also bend his or her knees, as he or she progressed down the row. Sometimes the strain on the back was so intense it caused pickers to crawl their rows, a process that somewhat eased their back pain but at the expense of their knees. Dragging the sack in which the golf-ball-sized cotton bolls were carried added to the difficulty of an already challenging job. The Texas sun, with a healthy dash of humidity thrown in, offered an unabated assault on the pickers that took a heavy toll on them. The ever-present dust clung to their sweaty bodies adding to their discomfort. On any given day, a good picker was expected to pick around 300 pounds of cotton. Pickers of average productivity would normally pick between 100 and 200 pounds per day. Hands down, Papa was the best picker in the family and maybe in all of Hamilton County, and Aub and Bon were not far behind him.

When Polly got her strength back from giving birth to Homer, she and all the kids headed to the cotton fields to help with the harvest. Baby Homer was put in a wicker basket, sometimes called a crib basket, and taken to the field at dawn each day. A piece of cloth covered the infant to keep him from frying in the Texas sun or inhaling too much dust. The cloth was moistened if the heat was intense. Additionally, the Eubanks family protected their skin from the scorching ultraviolet rays by smearing clay on their exposed skin. Polly placed the basket at the end of a row where it stayed until that row had been picked of its cotton. The basket was then moved over two rows until Polly had picked the next two rows. This process allowed her to check on her new baby every few minutes and feed him when he started fretting. If Homer was ailing, Mama Polly took him inside the house and cared for him until he returned to good health.

Homer remained in his basket until he learned to escape it and crawl himself into trouble. Once he was mobile, he was left in the house under Vina's or Bon's watchful eye. When Homer started teething, he was given a plug of Papa's tobacco to chew on. This 1909 version of a teething ring kept Homer satisfied but gave him a tobacco chewing habit that he didn't shake until he was 12.

In the late 1800s and early 1900s, parents of teething babies flocked to a product called Mrs. Winslow's Soothing Syrup. While it promised relief from teething woes, it, in fact, gave rest to the baby but not relief. It was ultimately discovered that it was nothing more than a cocktail of morphine and alcohol. In rural areas, many believed rubbing the gums with the brains of a hare would "cure" teething ills. In Tennessee, lots of folks believed rubbing the gums with a minnow would be curative. All these folk cures, along with others such as gnawing on corn cobs, knotted rags dipped in honey, and wooden beads eventually gave way to the pacifier. For Homer, gnawing on Red Indian Cut Plug did the trick.

One-year-old Homer-1909

Like his brothers and sisters before him, Homer began working in the fields when he was four or five. The first job for kids working in the fields was to bring water to the more productive pickers. When Papa decided the youngster was big enough and strong enough to work the rows, he or she passed the water delivery job down to the next in line.

Vina married her school boyfriend, the handsome Irishman Lee O'Bannon, in 1914. The newlyweds lived in Hamilton which enabled the 18-year-old Vina to maintain her stranglehold on discipline within the Eubanks household. Even with Vina out of the house, it was still so crowded there was simply no room inside for five of the Eubanks boys. Because he was so young, Cecil got to sleep in the house — at least for a few years. Aub, Ab, A.T., Paul, and Homer slept in the backyard on a row of iron cots in the warm months and in the barn during chilly months or on rainy nights. If the weather turned unbearable, they slept on the floor in the house. The brothers slept each night until the sunrise painted their faces with brightness and the crickets quit chirping. In Texas, the male crickets chirped from sunset to sunrise, rubbing their hind legs together to serenade the female crickets. This cacophony of cricket love songs started each spring and went on until the first frost, usually sometime in mid-October each year.

The outdoor cots the boys slept on were about 25 feet from the back door. They were lined in a row near the nexus of where three well-worn paths formed outside the back door. One path led to the outhouse, one to the barn, and one to the fields. Each cot came with a pillow and two blankets or quilts, or one of each. On particularly cool nights, the boys learned to situate their covers so that they didn't drag the ground. They did so to make it harder for scorpions to crawl up under the covers to enjoy the warmth they provided. The boys also learned to shake out their shoes or boots each morning before sticking their feet into them to dislodge any unwelcome guests that may have used them for sleeping quarters. At bedtime, the boys were careful to vigorously shake out their covers before snuggling under them, again to rid them of spiders, scorpions, and other critters.

Farming the land the Eubanks family operated under a sharecropping contract was the poor family's attempt at being self-sufficient. The 35 inches of annual rainfall that fell in Hamilton County seemed to be just enough to allow local farmers to complete their crops. At any one time, they had three or four milk cows, a couple of plow mules, and, of course, their pony, Old Dan. Papa had built a rather large hen house onto the side of the barn that housed about 15 layers. Papa also kept a small flock of guineas that ran free throughout the farm. These black and white speckled birds always impressed the young Homer with their work ethic and utility. While guineas are technically game birds and are rather wild, they pretty much stayed on task and they truly earned their keep on the farm. Though their small eggs were quite tasty, their primary function on the farm was to kill and eat mice, rats, and insects. They were so good at their jobs that farmers turned them loose in their produce and cotton fields because they devoured the insects that threatened their crops. The multi-talnted guineas mixed well with chickens and provided ear-piercing alarms when predators such as foxes, coyotes, and weasels neared the hen house in search of a meal. They also provided a measure of protection from snakes by harassing them until they slithered away in search of refuge from the irritating birds. The boys sleeping in the backyard felt safe because they knew the guineas would sound the alarm if trouble approached.

About three times a year, the farmers of Hamilton County gathered for jackrabbit roundups. These events almost took on carnival-like atmospheres, involving all members of the community, regardless of sex or age. The purpose of the roundups was to rid the land of as many jackrabbits as possible. Jackrabbits are hares, not rabbits at all. They were given the name "jackrabbits" by the first white settlers to Central and West Texas because they looked like rabbits with jackass ears. They roamed the countrysides of Central and West Texas in such large numbers they were major problems for farmers. The Texas Department of Agriculture noted that 128 of these long-eared critters consumed as much vegetation as one cow or seven sheep. A drove of jackrabbits could–and did–wipe out gardens or crops in no time.

Those participating in a roundup formed a large, close-knit circle and shrunk the circle gradually as they forced the hares to the center. Those in the circle carried clubs, hoes, shovels, or any other implement that could be used to beat the jackrabbits to death. Hundreds of the hares were killed at each roundup. It's debatable as to whether the roundups had any impact on the jackrabbit population, but, at least, the farmers and ranchers felt as though they were fighting for their land and crops. If organizations concerned with the prevention of cruelty to animals even existed in the 1910s, their scope of influence did not reach into rural Texas. Homer, and his brothers before him, began participating in these roundups when they were big enough to swing a club.

Very few of the farm families ate jackrabbits because the hares were notorious carriers of an infectious disease called tularemia. If contracted, tularemia attacked the skin, the eyes, the lymph nodes, and the lungs. It also caused the sufferer to run a high ever. Without antibiotics, the ones with the disease could die. Even with antibiotics, the disease could take up to three weeks to overcome. Jackrabbits also frequently suffered from bacterial and parasitic infection.

The family was a team, and each member seemed to know his or her responsibilities. This family teamwork got stronger and stronger as the years passed and the Eubanks kids became adults. The family was forever bound by an unspoken credo that translated to "when one Eubanks has a problem, all Eubankses have a problem."

## Storm Clouds over Hamilton

After Homer's birth in 1908, the Eubanks Family added a son, Cecil Raymond, in 1911, and a daughter, Phyllis Faye, in 1913. She was the last of Polly's and Robert's nine children. Aub married his longtime sweetheart, Grace Embrey, in 1917, and moved down the road to Burkburnett, Texas. That same year, Papa added 60 acres to the land he farmed. Things were clicking along nicely for the family, but ominous storm clouds were gathering.

As the war in Europe was winding down, a new and deadlier enemy reared its ugly head in America's wheat lands when the small, rural Southwest Kansas County of Haskell reported an outbreak of influenza grossly disproportionate to the county's size. From its humble beginnings in January of 1918, the virulent strain of flu–often referred to as the Spanish Influenza-stampeded through all of the nations of the world, ultimately leaving more than 50 million dead in its wake. Scientists have long debated where it began, but most say it started in China. Others say it began in Kansas, while British scientist J. S. Oxford maintained it began in a British Army post in France in 1916. Wherever it began, a full 20% of the world's population was infected.

In October of 1919 alone, the vicious virus killed 195,000 Americans, a staggering figure when one considers that the United States lost "only" 116,700 soldiers in all of World War I. By the time it had run its course in the winter of 1920, estimates were that it had claimed between 550,000 to more than a million Americans. One of those Americans to succumb to the deadly disease was Polly Anna (Ann) Davis Eubanks of Hamilton, Texas. She was 45 years old, wife to Robert A. Eubanks, and mother to nine children.

Polly's obituary that appeared in the Hamilton Record following her death on September 12, 1919, read in part:

> "...Polly and her husband, Robert A. Eubanks, had nine children, all of whom were present when Heaven claimed her sweet spirit. Fulfilling to the highest station the holy relations of wife and mother, this good woman was loved by her husband and children as few women are loved.
>
> On June 12, she fell ill suddenly and seriously. She was conveyed to Provident Sanitarium in Waco, where she underwent two surgical operations. Everything that physician and surgeon could suggest, and that loving hearts and willing hands could administer was employed in the effort to restore the beloved woman to health. No one ever fought more bravely or believed more unswervingly that life's span would be lengthened than she, but never a thought of herself, she only wished to be spared and restored in health to her loved ones. On Friday, just as the day was dying, her soul quietly left her poor, tired, suffering body and went to its true home–Heaven.
>
> The Hamilton Record would join the host of friends of the departed and her family in extending the comfort of sincere sympathy to those walking in the deep shadows of sorrow and loneliness."

After Polly's funeral, Papa and the kids returned to their farmhouse. The house soon overflowed with friends, family, and the foods the visitors brought to help the family through the next few days. Papa sat in a straight-back oak chair near the front door and nodded to and softly thanked those who came and went throughout the day. He seemed calm, but, in truth, he was tortured by Polly's death, angry at God, and overwhelmed by the devastation his Polly's death would inflict on his family.

While most of the children wore their grief on their faces, 11-year-old Homer mostly just stared at the floor and stayed to himself. At one point, he took his dazed and confused younger siblings, Cecil, 8, and Phyllis, 6, into their mama's bedroom and put his arms around them as they sat quietly on the floor in the corner. It was as though he realized Mama's death would be hardest on the two youngest, and that he–like all of his older brothers and sisters–would have to share in the raising of Cecil and Phyllis. While Homer's attention to Cecil and Phyllis was heartwarming and somewhat comforting, the act of tenderness gave disguise to the seeds of anger and toughness that were planted deep inside the young Homer by the passing of his mother–seeds that took root and complicated many parts of his life throughout his remaining years. The tough little tobacco-chewing boy seemed to steel himself for the hard times the tragedy had thrust upon him and his family. Like his papa, Homer, too, was angry over his mother's death.

The loss of a key family member leaves no choice for those left behind but to carry on as best they can, and that's what the Eubankses did. They carried on, but without the gentle hand and efficiency they had enjoyed under Polly's direction.

Papa, Ab, A.T., and Bon returned to the fields, while Paul, Homer, Cecil, and Phyllis returned to Freeman School #61, which was a few miles south of Hamilton, to work toward their completion of the seven grades taught in the one-room country school.

Homer at Freeman School, Hamilton, Texas (top row, fifth from the left)

Homer and friend on Old Dan at Freeman School in Hamilton

Edgar Bynum Pruitt was the only teacher at Freeman and taught all seven grades. Of course, Paul and Homer still had to work the fields during prime planting and harvest times.

Papa struggled. He went through the motions of fatherhood, farming, and living, but his energy, determination, sense of humor, confidence, and attention span weakened under the weight of his Polly-less life. It was obvious to his kids, other family members, and friends, that Robert was in trouble. The jobs of farming and raising kids clearly were overwhelming him. He was lonely, dispirited, and he was failing. Robert needed help.

Robert and Polly's families lived mostly in Arkansas, primarily the Fort Smith area. When word of Robert's downward spiral reached Arkansas, his and Polly's families launched an effort to get him to load up his family and bring them back to Arkansas where they could help him and his kids get a fresh start, a fresh start free from the heavy shadows cast by Polly's passing. Papa left the kids under Vina's care and went to Fort Smith for a look about.

The trip back home seemed to rejuvenate Papa, and he found strength in being near his kinfolks in Arkansas. Within two weeks of his return to Fort Smith, he had found 150 acres of fertile, rich farmland in the Arkansas River Valley, just west of the river that formed the border between the two states in Le Flore County, Oklahoma. It was love at first sight, and he secured farming rights to the land from the landowner under a sharecropping contract. Papa happily agreed to farm cotton. At that time, Oklahoma ranked fourth among cotton-producing states, so it fit in quite comfortably with Robert's years as a cotton farmer in Texas. The farm was in an area of the river bottom known as Peno Bottom. It was two miles southeast of Arkoma, 14 miles to Fort Smith, and 27 miles to the county seat of Poteau.

More excited than he had been since losing Polly, Papa headed back to Hamilton to uproot his children from the only home they had ever known and moved them to Peno Bottom, Oklahoma.

## Peno Bottom, Oklahoma, 1920

The relocation of the Eubanks Family from Hamilton, Texas, to Peno Bottom, Oklahoma, seemed to snap Papa out of his numbing depression. He busied himself getting the farmhouse in shape for the six of his children that made the move from Texas to Oklahoma. Family members from Arkansas crossed the Arkansas River to help Robert and his kids whip the house, barn, and fields into shape. The high level of activity put a spring back in Robert's step, but it was the richness of the soil that genuinely sent his blood racing.

During one of their first days at their new farm, Papa took all the kids out into the field and had them fill their hands with the fertile dirt and inhale its earthy aroma as he proclaimed that it was the richest soil he had ever seen. Seeing and sensing their papa's newfound energy put a charge into the six kids and definitely helped them adjust to their new surroundings. Meeting and getting to know their Arkansas cousins, aunts, and uncles also had a positive and calming effect.

Many families from the local farming community came by during their first few weeks to welcome the newcomers to the area, get acquainted, and offer their help in settling in. As was the custom, they also brought pies, fried chicken and other local delicacies. When the visiting families brought their children, Bonnie and Phyllis took right up with the girls. When the visitors brought boys, there was always a quiet, dirt-pawing time while they sized each other up, but new friendships were formed. The Seeber kids, who lived on the adjacent farm, agreed to walk to school with Paul, Homer, Cecil, and Phyllis the next morning since the Eubanks kids didn't know where the school was. Bonnie tagged along with them to make certain they registered and met the teacher, Mr. Vancil. Bon also packed an empty lard can with enough biscuits, ham, butter and molasses to get the kids through lunch. A. T., who had finished the eighth grade in Hamilton, was considered a graduate and stayed home to work the land alongside Papa.

Mr. Vancil, who was principal, teacher, and disciplinarian, always wore a three-piece wool suit. He welcomed the new students and gave them a ten-minute orientation, during which he outlined his expectations, his rules, and his willingness to punish those who fell short of meeting his standards. First-grade students through eighth-grade students shared the same teacher and same classroom. The students generally ranged from age six to age sixteen, although older kids often sat in just to get out of a day's hard work on the farm.

When the class was dismissed for lunch–or dinner, as it was called then – the Eubanks kids and the Seeber kids settled under a Bois D'Arc tree and started taking their food out of their syrup buckets. Their first day at school was off to a good start, and they had just begun eating when the largest boy in class, a fellow named Hooper, and two of his buddies strolled up to the gathering and told the Eubankses and the Seebers to move along because they were sitting where he and his friends wanted to sit. Hooper was red headed, freckled, clad in a faded pair of bib overalls, and mammoth. His menacing scowl added to his unpleasant and threatening appearance. His support team included a boy named Calvin and a lanky, tow-headed kid everyone called "Snag," probably due to his oversized, protruding front teeth. It was obvious Hooper was asserting his schoolground dominance over the new kids. Per the Seeber kids, Hooper had ruled the roost for several years, and he made his intentions to continue doing so quite obvious. In response to this ominous threat, Cecil, Phyllis, and the Seebers started packing-up their lunches in preparation for moving on. Homer and Paul just kept eating, and Homer told the others to stay where they were. A surprised Hooper repeated his "orders" in a louder voice, stepped closer to Homer, and told the stubborn newcomer he would drop him down the well if he didn't get a move on. Homer looked up at the towering menace and slowly got to his feet. Paul, also, stood and stepped between Hooper and his two minions. Phyllis started crying, Cecil looked confused, and the Seeber kids just hugged each other. The air was charged with friction awaiting the next action.

Homer only stood about chest-high to the bully, but he squared his shoulders, steadied his stance, and unleashed three quick blows to Hooper's face. The big fellow wiped at the blood dripping from his nose and lunged at the smaller, faster boy, but to no avail. Homer spun him around and peppered him three more times, dropping Hooper to his knees. His two buddies were paralyzed by what they had just seen and totally surrendered their aggression in front of the now emboldened Paul. They likely assumed that if one of these Eubanks boys could fight like that, the other one probably could, too. Hooper was whipped. The fight was over. Homer helped the big fellow to his feet and propped him against the tree, where the near-lifeless big fellow promptly slid down the trunk until his butt hit the ground.

When Mr. Vancil rung the bell signaling the lunch break was over, Homer helped Hooper up the steps into the classroom where all of the kids stared in disbelief at the scene that played out before them. As they were returning to their seats, Mr. Stancil asked Homer to step outside with him. Fearful he was about to be punished for fighting, Homer slowly followed the teacher outside. Instead of punishing him, Mr. Stancil told Homer he had watched the entire event and complimented him on his fighting prowess. Homer was never bullied again after the Hooper episode. He and Hooper even became friends, but there was never any doubt about who the king of the roost was now.

One morning when the Eubanks kids were walking to school, an over-sized red-headed girl grabbed little Phyllis by the arm and made her surrender her syrup bucket and the lunch that was inside it. Homer was quite a way ahead of Phyllis on the road but heard his little sister hollering and ran back to her. The large girl had the lard can pressed against her chest with one hand while she held Phyllis by the neck with her other paw. When she saw Homer running toward her, she narrowed her eyes and firmed-up her grips on both the bucket and the frightened little girl. She defiantly refused Homer's order to release Phyllis and hand over the lunch. When Homer reached for the bucket, the girl swung it at his head and scored a glancing blow. She then shoved Phyllis away and lit into Homer. She landed several blows before he regained control of the situation. She was like an enraged bull, so, as a last resort, Homer slugged her upside the head. The fight was over and Phyllis got her lunch back. That story is worth telling because the hungry, hard-fighting, red-headed juggernaut was Lois, Hooper's younger sister. Homer decided right then that trouble just runs in some families. He also conceded to Paul later that day that he would rather fight Hooper than Lois. He thought Lois was filled with evil spirits, and her eyes spooked him.

A few months after her near-traumatic encounter with Lois, Phyllis was trailing Paul, Homer, and Cecil on the way home after school when something happened that sent her running past her brothers with tears streaming down her cheeks. The boys tried to slow her down and find out what her problem was, but the little brunette with the short hair just darted right past them and ran the rest of the way home. She was still sobbing when she got home and went straight into her and Bon's bedroom where she flopped face down on their bed. Bon, who had basically become a mother to Phyllis when their mother died, followed her little sister to comfort her and try to help solve her problem. After much coddling and coaxing, the seven-year-old Phyllis revealed to Bon that she was now pregnant and didn't want to be. It seems a young classmate of Phyllis's had the sweets on her, and, while walking home from school with her, had kissed her on the cheek. Somewhere along the way, Phyllis had heard that kissing would make you pregnant and, in her mind, she had just been impregnated by her infatuated classmate. Bon's patient explanation of what actually caused pregnancy totally confounded the innocent young girl, but also, greatly relieved her. Shortly after that educational moment,

Phyllis hopped off the bed and rushed off to tell Cecil where babies came from.

Homer finished Peno Bottom School when he was 14 and had completed the eighth grade. He and Mr. Vancil remained friends for many years. Phyllis finished high school in Arkoma, and moved to Lubbock, Texas, where she lived with her brother Ab and his wife, Pearl, while she attended Texas Tech University, which was then known as Texas Tech College.

## Homer's First Kiss
## and
## Near Drowning

The busiest time on the farm was when the cotton was in bloom and ripe for picking. It was all hands on deck, six or seven days a week during the picking season, which in Peno Bottom usually began in late September and ran into late October. After all the cotton was picked and sent to the gin, the field, or fields, had to be turned over every year to prevent diseases and to limit boll weevil invasions.

New seeds were planted each year and the planting season was also labor intensive. It generally occurred from mid-March to the end of June. Peno Bottom had near-ideal cotton soil because it was loose, rich, and drained well. The average annual rainfall of 48 inches was ample for the health of the plants, and the cotton plants easily got the required four to five hours of direct sun daily.

When planting and picking were completed, the kids of cotton farmers had some free time to manage. The options for activities were rather limited due to a lack of money, limited transportation, the sparsity of neighbors, and the considerable distances to nearby towns, but rural farm kids, including the Eubankses, found things to do and the time and means to do them.

When the Eubanks boys got old enough to go courting, they had to beat their brothers to Little Dan as he was the only means of transportation available to them. Many arguments broke out over who was entitled to use Little Dan. In Hamilton, they had had a pony named Old Dan, but Papa had sold it before moving to Peno Bottom. Once they were settled into their new home, Papa had bought them another small horse which they promptly named Little Dan. Little Dan was brown and had the look of a wild mustang with a generous mane. He had an outsized clump of hair between his ears that looked as though it had been combed down toward his eyes. The stocky Little Dan was somewhat of an independent rascal who occasionally would buck his rider off for no apparent reason. The boys tried to break the pony of his intemperate behavior but, in the end, it was the boys who had to adjust to Little Dan, not the other way around. Little Dan seemed to hang onto some of his winter coat year-round, as patches of longer, thicker winter hair stayed scattered around his muscular little torso throughout the summer. It wasn't a good look, but perfection took a backseat to utility in Peno Bottom.

One spring day at school, Homer surrendered to his infatuation with his beautiful classmate, Millie O'Tomlin, and asked her for permission to "come calling" Saturday evening. His surprising boldness was clearly the result of his having been overcome by Millie's beauty, causing him to blurt out his question before he had time to talk himself out of doing so. As soon as he had asked the question, he felt as though his face was on fire and he was consumed by his need for fresh air. As it was only Tuesday when Homer asked for, and received, permission to come for a visit, he had four days left to worry about how he should handle his date; and worry he did. He had barely even spoken to girls before and had never really talked to one for more than a minute or so. What would he say? Wracked by doubts about his ability to follow through on his date, he thought about running away from home, sending a message to Millie that he was sick, or sending word to her that Little Dan had broken his leg leaving him no way to get there. The teasing he took from his siblings only added to his stress level that already had him on the verge of hiding in the barn.

Saturday finally came, so it was time for Homer to do the honorable thing and call on Millie. With Bon's help, Homer decked out in his finest clothes and combed his unruly hair as best he could. Bon put some kind of grease on the back of his head in an effort to plaster down his ever-present rooster tail and trimmed the wayward hairs on his neck and above his ears. Paul—perhaps feeling guilty for the ribbing he had given his younger brother over his romantic evening—saddled Little Dan and had him waiting for Homer in front of the house. Homer mounted his pony, waved sheepishly to his family, and rode off as though he was on his way to the gallows. It was a little over four miles from his house to Millie's house. He wished it were 30 miles. He had Little Dan walking so slowly, the bored horse stopped and dozed off a few times.

Despite all of his foot-dragging, the bashful Homer ultimately arrived at Millie's front porch. Much to his chagrin, Millie was nowhere in sight. Her Pa, however, was sitting in the porch swing just barely swinging. The swing groaned an ear-piercing screech that sent goose bumps running up and down Homer's spine. The noise it made was first cousin to the sound a fingernail on a blackboard makes, and the dirge it was emitting further unsettled the nervous young courter. Mr. O'Tomlin, who spoke with traces of an Irish accent, rose and enthusiastically shook Homer's hand. He then initiated a small-talk conversation about farming, the weather, and how Homer's family was. Homer was just beginning to feel more comfortable when Mr. O'Tomlin told him to have a seat while he fetched Millie. The "what do I do now?" moment was fast approaching.

When Millie came through the front door, Homer remembered why he was so smitten. She was dressed to the nines and looked stunning in her blue and white gingham dress and matching blue ribbons that decorated her hair. He just wanted to stare at her and was wishing he didn't have to talk. Perhaps because her beauty had taken him a bit by surprise, he couldn't think of a single thing to say. She took his hand and invited him to walk with her. The handholding and the intoxicating smell of her lilac water were very nice, but they didn't help him think of anything to say. He basically just answered her questions and let her lead him around the farm. When they came to the edge of their stock pond, Millie stopped and commented on how beautiful the moon was. Her delicate small voice was nearly drowned out by the cacophony of jumbled night sounds from excited crickets, bull frogs, coyotes, and owls. Homer's throat was too dry to answer her, so he just nodded his agreement. As he was doing so and staring up at the moon, Millie kissed him on the cheek. He dang near fainted.

He then looked into her eyes and found a sweetness and softness that inspired him to kiss her on her cheek. Even though he rushed this kiss, it was almost an out-of-body experience for him and he was shocked he had done it. His derring-do both surprised and embarrassed Homer. To his way of thinking, this two-kiss encounter had yielded results far greater than he ever expected. Surmising that nothing else could occur that would improve his first date, and still struggling for words, the shy–yet fulfilled–lover announced to Millie that he had to be getting home. He, and a somewhat confused Millie, headed back to the house. Once there, Homer went straight to Little Dan and climbed in the saddle. As he turned Little Dan toward the road, he looked over his shoulder and asked if he could come back again. She nodded "yes" and smiled at him as he disappeared into the dark. His entire visit had lasted less than 30 minutes. Even so, he was intoxicated by the onrush of emotions his romantic encounter with Millie had caused. He felt as though his heart was about to jump out of his chest, and he was certain his face was glowing a bright red. He wondered if these new feelings and sensations meant he was in love.

Homer did return for more visits to Millie's house, and he eventually reached the point at which he could talk, laugh, and enjoy longer visits. It's not known for sure how this romance progressed or how long it lasted, but it lasted long enough for Homer to find out he could actually feel comfortable around girls.

Like most country kids, the Eubanks boys and girls had found a swimming hole near their house where they could take a cooling dip on hot, humid days. In essence, the swimming hole was a wide spot in a creek that ran year-round. It was big enough to actually swim in and deep enough to dive in from a high bank on one side and an overhanging oak limb on the other. Other farm kids in Peno Bottom, also, laid claim to the swimming hole, so it was a summer gathering spot of sorts.

One summer day, a long, hard downpour had swollen the swimming hole so much that it escaped its banks. The normally peaceful waters were quickly beset by eddies, stampeding debris from upstream and a swiftness of current seldom witnessed before. As was usually the case, when the rainstorm moved on, the skies brightened, the birds turned chirpy, and the Eubanks boys were looking for adventure.

Paul and Homer decided to visit the swimming hole for a storm inspection and, perhaps, a dip in the cooling waters. They were taken aback by the size of their spot and the intimidating power of the creek's rushing water. With a keen sense of trepidation and an unspoken knowledge that they shouldn't go near the water, the brothers decided to go upstream, jump in, and let the fast-moving water carry them down to their familiar swimming hole. The instant they were in the roiling water, they realized they had little or no control over the direction the water was taking them or the speed with which it was doing so. It was too late to back out, so the boys fought the urge to panic and began to do what they could to control their out-of-control adventure.

The current bounced them off of newly submerged tree limbs, bushes, and rocks, but they both managed to keep their heads above water enough to breathe. When they reached their old swimming hole, the swift current refused to let them escape to dry land. They were about 12 feet apart when Paul saw Homer sucked beneath the surface. Paul eventually grabbed onto a sturdy bush and put a stop to his futility. He looked around desperately for Homer but could not see him. He re-joined the racing current, thinking Homer may have re-emerged further downstream. He hadn't. Homer had been sucked under the raging waters and had been slammed into an old submerged broken-up buckboard wagon that the rising waters had engulfed.

The wagon seemed to have reached out and grabbed Homer's leg, trapping him underwater. Homer could tell his foot was jammed into an old wagon wheel and his efforts to free it were useless. Dangerously short on air, Homer stopped trying to free his foot and turned his attention to breaking the wheel away from the rickety wagon. He braced his free foot against the side of the wagon, grabbed the top of the wheel that imprisoned him, and, with all the strength he could muster, pulled the wheel until half of it broke away from the axle. He was still imprisoned by the spokes of the half of the wheel that had broken away but was able to hold onto the wagon and use it to work his way up to the water's surface.

Once he had caught his breath and calmed himself, he crawled onto the slippery bank with the help of some sweet gum tree roots and wrestled his foot free from the wheel. Homer would forever remember this harrowing experience as the most frightening event of his life. He occasionally had nightmares about the incident well into his adulthood.

The walk home was slow and silent, as both boys knew they had narrowly escaped a near life-ending event. They vowed never to pull such a stunt in the future. As they neared home, Homer tried his best to suppress his limp, not wanting to have to explain to Papa how he had got it. Bon noticed his slight limp, but Papa didn't.

## Going to Town with Papa

When the Eubanks Family lived near Hamilton, Saturdays often meant trips to downtown Hamilton for the entire family. Mama and the older girls would do their grocery and dry goods shopping, and Papa would often sell fresh produce from his garden. He would also drop by the local saloon for a few beers and fellowship with the other men of the area. The boys gathered with other area boys outside the mule barn on the northeast side of town, about two blocks off the town square. Its location was in deference to the prevailing Southwestern wind that carried its stink away from town.

On a calm day, the boys just sat around talking and, occasionally sneaking smokes. Other days, when the boys struggled for higher positions on the totem pole, they broke out in wrestling, foot racing, arm wrestling, and, of course, fist fighting. Even though young, Paul established his prowess in both wrestling and foot speed. Homer was well known for his ability to hold his own in fights with boys several years older than he was. Few boys in his age group wanted to tangle with the boy whose papa once described him as a tornado wrapped in barbed wire.

After the family buried Mama Polly and moved to Oklahoma, Papa continued loading his family into the buckboard and taking them to town with him on Saturdays. Bon and Phyllis took over the grocery buying, Papa continued his "spit and whittle" sessions with the other men, and the boys continued to gather with other area boys; only this time, when they went into Arkoma, they met up behind the local feed and seed store. Most of the area boys got along just fine with each other, so fighting and racing were seldom on the agenda.

Arkoma was only two miles from the Eubanks' farm and Fort Smith was 14 miles from it. Most Saturday town visits were to

Arkoma, but, about once a month, Papa took the family to Fort Smith for a family visit with both the Eubankses and his in-laws, the Davises. The Fort Smith visits were overnight affairs to which all the kids looked forward. The city had a population of close to 30,000 and it was full of hustle, energy, and laughter most Saturdays. Garrison Street in downtown Fort Smith often took on a carnival-like atmosphere on those days.

Bon and Phyllis spent much of their time in downtown window shopping and wishing. Their lack of money relegated them to just looking, but it was fun for them to see the fashions of the day and imagine themselves decked out in the fashion fineries. They also enjoyed watching the electric streetcars and were occasionally treated to a ride on one by their uncle Claude.

The boys enjoyed seeing all of the "new" girls and hanging out with the local boys under the Arkansas River bridge. There was plenty of time for them to visit, but their day was more-or-less focused on the competitions held weekly for the boys. Fighting among the boys was organized, and many of the town folks gathered around to watch the fights and wager on them. The ring was defined by a circle drawn in the dirt. The object of the fight was to beat the opponent into submission or knock him out of the ring. There were no gloves, but there were rules. A competitor could be disqualified if he bit, clawed, kicked, threw dirt, or used a weapon of any sort. An adult volunteer provided the basics of refereeing. Organized foot races and horse races also took place, but the fighting got top billing. Paul won most of the foot races and Papa made more money betting on him than he did selling produce.

Homer was the designated Eubanks fighter. He fought well above his size and age, so Papa was usually able to place bets on his boy with good odds. No one knew where the scruffy kid's power came from, but it came hard and fast and usually left his opponent in a sobbing pile in the dirt in no time. Papa, who was a quiet man by nature, just smiled as he collected the money he won from Paul's and Homer's performances. He always shared his bounty with the boys by buying them a root beer at the Davis Drug Company.

The men who came to downtown Fort Smith on Saturdays had a number of choices in which they could participate. Papa joined other men in the park for talking, enjoying tobacco, cussing the government, and an occasional game of horseshoes. Also, one could always find a game of poker or dominoes if he were so inclined. Everything was calm and relaxed until word arrived that the boys had started racing and fighting. An air of urgency and excitement then swept through the park and it soon emptied out rather quickly as the men went to watch the action.

Homer might have inherited his toughness and fighting ability from his grandpa and great uncle on the Davis side of the family, both of whom traveled around Arkansas, Missouri, Western Tennessee, and Northeast Texas in the late 1800s as prize fighters. The fights in those days were not sanctioned and were often against the law, but they were a regular Saturday event in many smaller cities and towns. Like the boy-fights Homer participated in, the ring was defined by a circle drawn in the dirt street or on the floor of a spacious barn. The rules were also similar and the fight went on until one fighter couldn't answer the bell. The fighters got a small cut of the betting take, with the winner drawing the biggest share. Family lore had it that Grandpa Davis never lost a fight, but there were no formal records kept that would bear that out. That same family lore claimed that Grandpa Davis often won his fights by gouging his opponents eyes out of their sockets. Sometimes lore and truth don't look much alike, but, in this case, who knows?

Saturdays in town with Papa were grand diversions from the routine and tiresomeness of sharecropping that dominated the lives of the Eubanks kids. They were also part of the glue that bound this family into a solid unit, a glue that unified this sharecropping family with an unbreakable bond of love and mutual support throughout their lives and on into future generations.

## Papa Takes a Wife

The move to Peno Bottom had been good for Papa. The land was producing good cotton, his kids were comfortably settled in, and his visits with relatives across the state line into Arkansas seemed to feed his spirits. His walk had regained its zip, and his sense of humor was back in place.

The one downer in his life that fertile soil, loving kids, and family reunions couldn't fix was loneliness. He had accepted that Polly was gone, but he hadn't accepted the void in his life her absence had left behind. Papa wasn't looking to replace Polly in his heart, but he decided he did want to replace her in his bed, his kitchen, and in his effort to keep his family farm life running smoothly. A family farm just plain needed the presence and touch of a strong woman, so he set out to find one.

Papa didn't tell the kids of his plans to find a new wife. He didn't need to. The kids were very aware of the fact that Papa was spending more and more time in town. Plus, they noticed he was dressing better, shaving more often, and even leaving the house smelling of lilacs. The kids often quizzed Papa on his activities, but they never got any meaningful explanations. Instead, all they got were nods, grins and more whistling.

During his search for a new woman, Papa sought input about available women from his Arkansas kin, his Oklahoma farming buddies, and the local Methodist preacher. From one of these sources, the name Thelma Louise Brackenmeyer found its way to Robert's ear. Thelma, known simply as T. Lou, was widowed some time back, and left to make do on her own. She had two small children, and, like Robert, needed a partner to help her survive and raise her children.

T. Lou was a large-boned, square-shouldered woman who exuded strength, both physical and mental. Robert knew that if he married her, he would be in for a fight about just who wore the britches. On the other hand, he thought he needed a strong woman to help carry the load of raising kids and running the farm. Perhaps because there weren't many available women in the area, or perhaps because he knew he wasn't the greatest catch in the world for a needy woman, Papa zeroed in on T. Lou. Papa knew this big German woman came with a streak of meanness running through her veins. He also knew she would be disruptive to the lifestyle he and his kids had settled into, but he figured the good she could do outweighed the challenges she would bring.

After a five-month-long courtship, Papa and T. Lou married in a quiet service at the office of the Justice of the Peace in Poteau. They then loaded T. Lou's kids and belongings into the buckboard and headed for Peno Bottom. Papa was happy that he no longer would have to sleep in an empty bed. He was also happy that his iron-willed oldest daughter, Vina, had married and moved away. He knew that no house in Oklahoma would have been big enough to accommodate two women as controlling and dominant as T. Lou and Vina under its roof. As he thought of these two warriors under the same roof, he chuckled, shook his head, and calmly urged his team on down the road.

The Eubanks kids had never even heard T. Lou's name, much less met her, when Papa pulled the wagon up to the back door of their farmhouse. The kids slowly assembled around the wagon as Papa helped this strange woman and her two small children down from the buckboard. T. Lou stood erect and unsmilingly looked over the Eubanks kids and her new house. Her kids, a boy and a girl, stood behind their mama and peeped around her full-length skirt at their new family members.

After introducing his new bride and her children, Papa lined up Bon, Paul, Homer, Cecil, and Phyllis, and introduced them one at a time to the stoic, stone-faced woman. Bon decided right away that if her new stepmother had any warmth, it was packed away in one of her three suitcases. Homer noticed she was taller and more muscular than Papa, and he whispered to Paul that she could whip Papa in a fist fight. The ever-happy Cecil just stood there smiling as he held onto Paul's overalls. Phyllis hid behind Bon. This auspicious coming together of two families finally resulted in the three boys taking all of T. Lou's belongings inside and Papa leading his wife into her new house.

The first thing T. Lou did when she stepped into the house was inspect the kitchen and inventory the pots, pans, and utensils. She then opened a box she had brought with her and unpacked her own kitchen items. From the kitchen, she moved to the bedroom she would share with Papa. Lastly, but most intently, she inspected the sleeping quarters for the children. She then announced to all that the sleeping arrangements would have to be changed considerably to accommodate her two little ones.

It was a bit of a rough start for the merged families, one that was rather cold and emotionless, but the Eubanks kids knew it couldn't be wished away. Papa seemed happy and appeared to be unaware of his new wife's indifference to his kids and the drill-sergeant mentality she affected when dealing with them in his absence. Papa also failed to notice, or at least acknowledge, that T. Lou gave the best cuts of meat and larger shares of the food served at each meal to her two kids. The Eubanks kids were very aware of the preferential treatment her two kids were receiving, but they were clueless as to what to do about it. Their efforts to explain the situation to Papa fell on deaf ears. Paul surmised that her performance in the bedroom obviously carried more weight with Papa than did his own kids' cries of injustice. The kids, more or less, settled into the second-class status to which their new stepmother had relegated them. Well, all of them did except Homer.

Papa's relationship with T. Lou may have been on solid ground, but the relationship between Homer and T. Lou was anything but. T. Lou had a volcanic temper and Homer's defiance triggered it often. Whatever she was peddling, Homer wasn't buying. Papa, aware of the strife between his wife and son, refused to involve himself at any level. As the months passed, the conflict between the two intensified, finally reaching its boiling point one night at supper time. Before T. Lou could serve her two kids, Homer took the skillet from the stove and served his brothers and sisters first. He then served his two step-siblings and returned the skillet to the stove. There was a pronounced silence around the table as those seated there stared on in amazement at Homer's breach of T. Lou's protocol. Even Papa was stunned into silence.

T. Lou then yanked the meat off of Homer's plate and put it on her children's plate. Homer jumped up to retrieve it when his angry stepmother took the iron skillet in hand and swung it at Homer's head. Homer was too fast for her and grabbed her wrist, stopping the blow. After causing her to drop the skillet, he backed her into the still-hot stove and held her there until it burned through her blouse and into the skin on her lower back.

Before the next round of the battle could begin, Papa forced Homer out of the backdoor and, more importantly, away from T. Lou. The rest of the Eubanks kids—in a show of unity—took their plates, along with Homer's, to the backyard where the Eubanks kids ate together. Before coming outside, Bon had taken Homer's meat from T. Lou's kids' plates. She returned it to her little brother.

Even though Homer was only fourteen at the time of this climatic event, he distanced himself from T. Lou and spent a lot of time visiting relatives in Arkansas and Texas. When he was at home, he slept in the barn.

The marriage between Papa and T. Lou produced two more Eubanks children, Lola Dean and Robert, Jr. Their marriage lasted until the kids were grown. Then they split up. Papa retired from farming and moved to Muskogee, where his youngest daughter, Lola Dean, helped take care of him. T. Lou lived well into her nineties. Homer never visited her. Nor did any of the original Eubanks kids attend her funeral.

## Birthday in a Box

The tension between the Eubanks kids and their stepmother grew daily, especially for Homer. His confrontation with her had led to her modifying some of the partiality she had always shown her kids at the expense of the Eubanks children. There was no mystery about what had caused her to "soften" her position toward the Eubankses. It wasn't inspired by a change of heart. It was inspired by her knowledge that Homer was closely watching her and that he would move against her if he found her impartiality waning. Simply put: she was afraid of Homer. She never feigned liking Homer and, if looks could kill, he would have been six feet under, but she gave him a wide berth. The fragile truce between Homer and T. Lou helped bring a modicum of peace to the house, but the Eubanks kids couldn't wait to leave home. The kids felt as though T. Lou had castrated their once fiery Papa and buried his balls behind the barn.

In 1923, A.T. and Paul had heard the wheat harvest in California needed more workers, so they moved in with relatives in Fort Smith from where they figured they could catch a ride westward to California. Their search for a ride to California led them to Tulsa, where they rode with a trucker hauling oilfield equipment to Long Beach. Within days of their arrival, they found work in the wheat fields. The wheat harvest started in Southern California and moved North as the Southern regions had been harvested. The wages were better than they could have made picking cotton in Oklahoma or Texas, plus the ranchers provided food and shelter for the workers.

Soon after their arrival, A.T. and Paul sent word for Homer to try to get to California where he could join them in the wheat fields. Homer latched on to this invitation from his brothers and saw it as his chance to break away from the animosity he and T. Lou shared toward each other. When he told Papa of his intentions to leave home, Papa half-heartedly tried to talk his 14-year-old into staying in Peno Bottom, but he understood Homer's situation and supported his plan. Bon took the separation from her little brother hard and when the time came for him to leave, she wept for three days. If she hadn't needed to take care of Cecil and Phyllis, she would have left home, too.

Homer was alone with a lot of miles between him and California. He decided he didn't want to hitch a ride in a car or truck to California but opted instead to hop a west-bound freight train. Trains fascinated him, and some of the older boys in Fort Smith had made hopping a freight sound easy and adventurous. They claimed to have done so many times, and Homer assumed they were telling him the truth. One of Homer's cousins had taken him to the Fort Smith & Western Railroad depot where they found a rail map of the United States. With his cousin's help, Homer chose to ride the FS&W to Oklahoma City. From there, he would check other maps and hide out on the train that got him most directly to Los Angeles.

On the morning he was set to hop a freight to OKC, Homer checked his cash and decided he could spare enough to buy breakfast at a diner located near the tracks. Eating out was totally new to him so he entered the half-full diner rather timidly and sat on a counter stool. He had seen a sign on the side of Jarman's Grocery in Fort Smith for a new-to-him breakfast food called "Post Toasties." He decided to try it, though he was nagged by a fear that he would make a fool of himself by ordering it since he didn't know for sure what it was. When the old, gum-smacking waitress asked him what he wanted, Homer softly answered, "a bowl of Post Toasties." She was either hard of hearing or hadn't paid attention to his order as she dang near hollered for him to speak up. Somewhat louder, he again ordered Post Toasties but, just as before, she hollered for him to quit mumbling and to speak up. Her response had caused other diner patrons to look at him and tune into the one-sided conversation going on between the tactless waitress and the shy country boy. At this point, Homer was not only embarrassed, he was hacked off. In response, he stood up and hollered back at her, "I want a damn bowl of chili!"

He would try Post Toasties when he got to California.

Homer stowed away in a boxcar on a train headed for Oklahoma City and had no problem avoiding detection from the railroad bulls. "Bulls" was a term attached to the railroad police by hobos of the early 20$^{th}$ century because of the no-nonsense–and often brutal–way they treated the ticketless riders. Riding the rails became a popular means of transportation for cash-strapped men and those who sought the cheapest means of traveling to new places, new jobs, and new adventures. These rail hoppers were called hobos, and the bulls found nothing acceptable about these freeloaders and worked hard to rid the rails of them. The bulls were generally armed with clubs and firearms, either of which they were quick to use to get rid of the hobos.

In OKC, an older veteran hobo befriended young Homer and took him to a nearby hobo camp where the young traveler was fed and given a place to bed down for the night. Instinctively, Homer knew he was in someone else's world and needed to be on guard, but he actually felt at ease with this band of broke travelers. By listening, he was able to pick up a lot of information that would come in handy as he continued his trek.

Among the useful information his new friends passed on to him was how to board a rolling train. They told him to find a slow-moving train, run along beside it, and grab on to the ladder on the side of a car as it rolled by. They told him to then let his legs fly behind him as the train pulled him off of his feet. With a firm grip on the ladder, he was to pull himself onto the train when his legs swung back toward the ladder. He understood their tutorial and used this method many times in the coming years.

Perhaps the most valuable information the veteran hobos shared with him was included in their discourse on the railroad bulls. They imprinted on him the danger of being caught by a bull, particularly while the train was rolling. They told Homer any bull would knock or throw him off the train if he was caught, and that they would often do so after administering a brutal beating with their nightstick. He was told to avoid capture any way he could, even if it meant jumping off of a moving train.

The next morning, Homer and several other hobos headed for the railyard. Once in sight of it, they went into stealth mode and worked hard to go unseen as each searched for the train he was looking for. With some difficulty, Homer found his train; one headed for Amarillo and points west. It looked to him like a straight shot from OKC to Los Angeles with a few stops along the way.

From Amarillo to Albuquerque to Flagstaff to Kingman to L.A. He wouldn't even have to change trains. What could go wrong?

Homer's trip was uneventful from Oklahoma City to Albuquerque where it stopped for a crew change and to add three or four cargo-laden cars heading to L.A. There was a cursory inspection of the train cars by a pair of railroad policemen, but Homer was able to hide himself among the many bags of fertilizer that almost filled his boxcar.

Once the train jerked itself taut and began rolling toward Arizona, Homer breathed a sigh of relief. The car in which he rode left both of its side doors open so fresh air could keep the somewhat volatile fertilizer from overheating. The open doors were a plus in Homer's mind because they gave him a backdoor if a bull entered his car and he needed a fast get-away. Not long after the freight train built its speed, the hypnotic noise made by the wheels on the track entranced the young hobo and he fell asleep. He roused up briefly as his train slowed down as it passed through Winslow, Arizona, but he quickly dozed back off when the train regained its speed.

Homer's dream state came crashing down with a violent thud when he found himself in the grasp of what, at that blurry moment, looked like the biggest man he had ever seen. A bull had found the sleeping young boy and had yanked him to his feet and initiated a beating all in one motion. The bull started the beating with a powerful backhand across Homer's right cheek, followed by a blow to his mid-section. As Homer bent over in pain, the bull pulled his nightstick from his belt and rendered Homer unconscious with a solid blow to the back of his head. The bull then dragged the unconscious Homer to the open door and threw him off the train.

When the unconscious boy hit the ground, he had apparently landed in a ravine face first. The badly injured Homer laid in the ravine for more than 24 hours before regaining consciousness. When he first opened his eyes, he could barely see light through the narrow slits in his badly swollen eyes. He remembered parts of the beating he had sustained, and he slowly realized the bull must have thrown him off the train. Though he ached all over, he was greatly relieved to learn his arms and legs seemed to be working okay; sore but usable. His head hurt horribly and he could barely swallow. He knew his face was badly swollen, and when he gently felt around his mouth, he discovered it was completely blood-encrusted and painful to the touch. The still-addled young man was startled and confused when he felt a sizable rock protruding from the area just above his left upper lip. With his tongue, he was able to feel the other end of the rock sticking out of the roof of his mouth. The rock was firmly set and refused to move when he tried to wiggle it. His tongue was also able to feel the gap where two of his upper teeth should have been, but it was the embedded rock that caused him the most concern. After this quick inventory of his sorry state, Homer came to the realization he had been impaled on the rock when he fell from the train.

The tough little Texan managed to get to his feet and steady himself. He knew he had to find civilization and medical attention before he could resume his trek to California. He crawled out of the ravine and more or less staggered up to the track bed and stood in between the glistening rails. He knew he was somewhere between Winslow and Flagstaff, but he wasn't really certain if he was closer to Winslow or to Flagstaff. He opted to head toward

Flagstaff, mainly because it was on the way to California.

The more he walked, the better his legs worked, and he was eventually able to hit a pretty decent stride. His head and his face continued to throb mercilessly, but he kept walking. He had no other options. After about an hour, Homer spotted a stock tank at the base of a windmill about a quarter of a mile north of the tracks. The water in the tank was a welcome sight for the stranded boy and he slipped through a poorly built barbed wire fence and headed straight for it. The tank stood at the edge of a stand of pinyon pines and junipers. A steady trickle of water pumped by the screeching, rusty windmill kept the tank about three quarters full. Deer and cattle hoofprints were all around the tank marking it as a well-used oasis in the Arizona high desert.

The first thing Homer did was to submerge his battered head into the cool water. He lightly rubbed his face, ridding himself of much of the dried blood that clung to the left side of his face. He then edged over to the water-yielding pipe, leaned down, and sucked up water his parched body so desperately needed. He had gone without food and water since he had a biscuit and a cup of water in Albuquerque. Homer then took off his shirt, soaked it in the water, and wrapped it loosely around his head hoping it would ease the relentless throbbing. Homer picked as many pinyon nuts as he could hold and devoured them while sitting in the shade of a pine. After grabbing a short rest, the traveler drank more water, re-stuffed his pockets with the nourishing nuts, and returned to his task at hand.

Homer walked for several hours more and stopped for a bit of sleep under the bright moon. At dawn the next morning, he ate a handful of nuts and trudged on toward Flagstaff. He had to get off the track twice to let highballing freight trains zip by him. Another stock tank and windmill allowed him to re-hydrate. He re-soaked his head, but the water still did nothing to alleviate his persistent headache or the fever he knew he had.

Despite his pain, Homer walked on into the night. After several more hours, his weariness was diminished greatly when he caught his first sight of what appeared to be the lights of a town in the distance. His fear that he was seeing a mirage turned to joy when he got close enough to see the lights did, in fact, signal he had reached civilization. He soon noticed a sign by the side of the track that signaled he was entering Flagstaff. The relief he felt added a new spring to his gait, and he was darn near running when he arrived at the stone rail station.

The injured young boy eased up the platform and peered in a window to see if anyone was about. There was one light coming out of an office near the back of the station. The light shone bright enough to allow Homer to see the clock on the wall in the small waiting room. It was 11:25 p.m.. The door was locked and Homer was uncertain whether he should knock on it or wait until the following morning to seek help. When he saw movement in the lighted office, Homer opted to knock on the door in hopes of getting the attention of the night agent.

At first, the man inside the station walked haltingly toward the door trying to discern who was interrupting his normally peaceful night shift. When the man got near the door, Homer told him he was injured and needed help. The still-cautious nightman opened the door and, after inspecting Homer, led him into his lighted office. In the light, he could tell Homer was just a kid and this seemed to relax him. The night man, whose name turned out to be Tiberius Barnes, was a small, bespeckled man in his 50s with thinning black hair he combed straight back. As he was inspecting Homer's battered face and gawking at the rock lodged just above his lip, Homer told his woeful story of what had led him to this point. As Barnes listened to the boy, he swung into action to try to treat his injuries.

He heated water and used it to clean Homer's wounds. He then applied some sort of mercury compound to the cuts and gashes on his face and shoulders. For the headache, Barnes mixed up headache powder for him. Finally, Barnes had addressed most of the boy's troubles except for the big one–the rock in his face. It was too late to get a doctor, so Barnes was faced with waiting until the morning or removing the rock as best he could. He chose to do the latter. He placed his left middle and index fingers inside Homer's mouth and gripped the rock protruding from outside his mouth with his right hand. As he pushed on the rock from the inside of the mouth, he pulled on the rock from the outside. However, the stone was firmly set and refused to budge. Barnes was fearful he had started a project he couldn't finish. As he pulled, he could see tears in his patient's eyes, though the boy never made a sound. Finally, the rock broke loose and, in sync, both Homer and Tiberius let out huge grunts of relief. As blood was gushing from Homer's wound, Barnes gave him a rag soaked in cold water and told him to hold it inside his mouth against the hole left by the rock's removal. He then filled the exterior wound with sulfa drugs and bandaged it.

While the worn-down Homer slumped against the wall in a modified state of shock, Barnes took a blanket and pillow from his office to a large cardboard box that was sitting on the dock outside the depot and made a bed for the young boy he had helped. After sharing his soup with Homer, Barnes took Homer to the box and told him to bed down for the rest of the night, saying he would return in the morning with the doctor. Homer had no problem going to sleep as his body had taken all of the trauma it could stand.

Early the next morning, Homer's deep sleep was disturbed by Barnes' gentle shaking of his shoulder. He crawled from his box to see Barnes and a man holding a small black bag. The new arrival was a local doctor by the name of L. W. Berry. Berry was a grey-haired man who looked to be in his 60s. His brow was wrinkled but his eyes were gentle and friendly. When he introduced himself to Homer, the boy's first response was to tell the doctor he had only $1.35, so he couldn't afford his services. Doc Berry's eyes never quit studying Homer's wounds, but as he was doing so, he told his tense young patient not to worry about the money. After a thorough examination, the threesome went in the station and the doctor re-cleaned Homer's wound with warm water and some kind of disinfectant. Next, he put six or seven stitches in the wound, doused it in mercurochrome, and covered his handiwork with a loose-fitting bandage. He told Homer to have the stitches removed in a week or so. He then told Barnes to keep him in Flagstaff a while longer and to call him if he had any problems.

With his meager funds, the repaired young traveler was able to buy a bowl of soup at a downtown café, which was all he could handle with his still-tender mouth. As Homer walked around the small town, he was surprised to learn that the story of his travails had been widely circulated among the citizenry. Apparently, his story had touched a few hearts in the rugged little town because several folks stopped him during his walk and offered him food and drink. The local barber, who was sitting on the sidewalk in front of his shop, coaxed Homer into a chair and gave him a free haircut. He also had his wife take the overwhelmed boy to their house for a bath. While Homer was bathing, the kindly lady took Homer's clothes and washed them. She then hung them outside to dry and gave Homer some of her husband's clothes to wear while he waited for his to dry. As he was killing time sitting in the barber shop, he noticed a calendar on the wall. He asked the barber what day it was, and when he found out it was October the 11th, he realized he had spent his 15th birthday, October 10th, sleeping in a box in Flagstaff, Arizona.

After getting into his clean clothes and returning the barber's clothes, he thanked the couple for the incredible kindnesses they had showed him. He continued his walking tour of Flagstaff.

After another night in the box, Homer was ready to move on to California. At mid-morning, a freight train bound for Los Angeles stopped briefly in Flagstaff to take on water. During that time, Tiberius Barnes talked the brakeman into letting Homer stow away in the caboose until they arrived in Los Angeles. After an awkward hug, during which the good Samaritan stuffed two dollars into the boy's shirt pocket, Homer and Barnes said their good-byes.

Homer would always remember Barnes and the people of Flagstaff for the way they took him into their hearts. The 15-year-old boy from Oklahoma had crammed a lot of learning about life into just a few days. Through the actions of the ferocious railroad bull, he had seen firsthand how mean and harmful some folks could be to others. Yet before the actions of the bull could taint his faith in his fellow humans, he had experienced the care, concern, and kindnesses of an entire town.

When Homer arrived in California, he contacted the company his brothers worked for. They told him the location of the crew and arranged for his ride to that location with a supplier that did work with the firm. The reunion between Homer, A.T, and Paul was joyous. A Mexican man in the crew who was called "Doc" removed Homer's stitches and re-bandaged his scar, and Homer worked the rest of the harvest in lockstep with his brothers.

## The Eubanks Kids Spread Out

When the wheat harvest in California was over, the boys were ready to head home. They had money in their pockets, a lot of new experiences under their belts, and a nodding acquaintance with manhood and life in general they didn't have when they started this great adventure. While A.T. and Homer had been inclined to spend their money on fun things in California, the level-headed Paul steered them away from wasting their hard-earned cash.

The boys were amazed at the differences of living in California versus Oklahoma and Texas. In the food department, the boys got their first-ever tastes of grapes, almonds, apricots, and something called an avocado. They saw mansions in Hollywood that were larger than the courthouses in rural Oklahoma and Texas. They saw more Mexicans in any one day than they had seen in their entire lives. They decided the girls in California were beautiful but weren't any prettier than those in Oklahoma. They were just better dressed, wore more make-up, smelled better, and were bolder. They saw fancy, expensive cars and no horse-or-mule-drawn wagons on the streets. Despite all of the remarkable differences they encountered, they were eager to get back to their old stomping grounds. So, after a couple of more swims in the Pacific and some trips to downtown Los Angeles for girl watching and related activities, the threesome headed to Texas. On their way back to Peno Bottom, they had decided to visit their brothers who lived in the longhorn state, Ab in Lubbock and Aub in Breckinridge.

They were able to hitch a ride on the back of a large truck and trailer that was hauling citrus and nuts to Albuquerque. They got rained on outside of Kingman, Arizona, but the trip was most tolerable, plus they were able to eat their fill of oranges, a delicacy they couldn't afford in Oklahoma. From Albuquerque, they hoboed to Amarillo on the Santa Fe Railroad and were undetected by any bulls. They took turns standing bull-watch and, needless to say, Homer was greatly relieved when they jumped off the train as it eased into the Texas city. They walked to the Southern edge of Amarillo and hitched a ride with a cattleman named Sparks. A.T. rode in the cab of the pick-up with Sparks, and Paul and Homer rode in the bed of the truck. Sparks took them all of the 124 miles to Lubbock and let them out in downtown. The ride took about three hours.

Lubbock was a dusty town of about 9,000 in 1924, but it was growing. Ab had married Pearl Tyler in 1921 and moved to west Texas town where he got a job as a typesetter at *The Avalanche-Journal*, a job he held for 49 years. Pearl worked at the local department store which was only three doors down from the newspaper office. The three brothers walked into the building and surprised Ab who was setting type in the back shop.

After work, Ab took his brothers to his favorite bar for drinks to celebrate their reunion. Ab was the smallest of the Eubanks boys, standing about 5'4" and weighing less than 100 pounds. Remarkably, he also had the deepest voice by far, a voice that should have been in a huge man, not the runt of the litter. Ab's size is important to the story because it rendered him unable to hold his liquor.

While sitting at the bar laughing it up with his brothers, Ab announced in his loud, deep voice that he smelled "har burnin'" (hair burning). After sniffing the air, the other boys agreed that, indeed, hair was burning and started trying to pin down the source of the problem. Homer, who was sitting next to Ab, noticed smoke rising from Ab's lap. It didn't take long for all to realize that their tipsy older-but-smaller brother's pants were on fire and the hair burning was pubic hair. They quickly dowsed the smoldering pants and accompanied Ab to the men's room to determine the extent of the damage. Apparently, the fire had fallen out of Ab's cigarette, burnt through his wool pants, and inflamed his private area. The pants-on-fire incident did little to slow down the fun the brothers were having, and they returned to the bar in full spirits.

Ab, perhaps emboldened by the presence of his three bigger and tougher brothers, began to get verbally aggressive with the other bar patrons. In fact, the snockered little fellow stood up, assumed his most intimidating stance, and hollered he could "whoop" any son-of-a-bitch in the joint. Most of the patrons knew Ab and ignored him, but just in case trouble was brewing, A.T. and Paul ushered Ab and Homer out of the bar. The 15-year-old Homer had had a few beers and was ready to join Ab in a housecleaning. When they got home, Pearl put Ab to bed, threw away his wool slacks, and fed the three road-weary brothers-in-law.

The reunion of brothers lasted three days before the traveling threesome made their way to Breckenridge, Texas, where they spent three days with their oldest brother Aub and his wife, the former Grace Embrey. Aub was working on an oil derrick in a new oil field, so he had to go to bed early and report to the rig at sunrise. The brothers crammed in a lot of visiting in the little time they had together and Aub seemed to eat up his time with his brothers. He had a rich sense of humor and laughed easily, so his brothers enjoyed his company, too. A.T. decided right then he wanted to work in the oilfields like Aub.

Just short of wearing out their welcome, the boys headed back to Peno Bottom, Oklahoma. Papa, Bon, Cecil, and Phyllis were ecstatic to have the three boys back home. T. Lou was polite and very pregnant with her and Papa's second child. Papa took the family to Fort Smith the following weekend for a family gathering at which the boys regaled the assembled family members with embellished stories of their great adventure. Homer's run-in with the railroad bull and the drama following it held the aunts, uncles, and cousins spellbound. Homer had always been a terrific storyteller. At the end of the session, Papa could be overheard telling his brother Claude, "I sent three boys off to California, and three men returned."

Now that Papa had his full workforce back at hand, the farm put together some of its best years. However, A. T. decided to move to Marshall, Texas which was booming as a railroad town, oil and gas center, and commercial hub. His oldest sister, Vina, and her husband, Lee, were prospering in Marshall. He was the manager of K. Wolens, the largest department store in Marshall and she ran its jewelry department. Vina's sisters and brothers said she worked at the store so she could fend off women who threw themselves at the handsome and suave Lee. Other women working at the store were deathly afraid of the hyper-jealous Vina and were extra careful not to do or say anything that she could construe as flirting with Lee.

Bon was eager to strike out on her own but Phyllis, who was more like her daughter than her little sister, came down with a near-fatal case of scarlet fever. The eleven-year-old Phyllis ran an exceptionally high fever for more than a week. The doctor from Arkoma visited her several times but was essentially ill-equipped to offer meaningful treatment. He told Bon and T. Lou to keep her head covered in cold rags and to try to get her to eat broth. He also left them a balm called nard which they were to put on a rag, steam, and place across her nose and mouth every four hours. Each time he left the sick little girl's side, he told the concerned family members the fever just had to run its course. Phyllis's fever finally broke and she slowly recovered from the draining illness. The family welcomed her back among the living but were startled to observe that Phyllis' hair had fallen out--all of the hair on her head except small patches above each ear and a small patch in the center of her forehead. Apparently, the high fever had burned up her hair follicles, and she was doomed to go through the rest of her life bald.

High fevers had been a major cause of death and illness for centuries. Ancient Romans had at least three temples dedicated to worshiping a god of fever. The invention of the mercury thermometer in 1714 by Daniel Fahrenheit gave doctors their first way to monitor rises and falls of fever. In 1900, medical experts decided there were three kinds of fever: yellow, typhoid, and scarlet. Yellow and typhoid were viral and were spread by mosquitoes. Scarlet, on the other hand, was bacterial and most cases were the result of the afflicted having strep infection in their throat.

Even in the 1920s, doctors who would treat rural people were scarce and were located primarily in the commercial center of an area. Therefore, home remedies were a medical mainstay on most farms. The Eubankses relied on a home remedy to try to regrow Phyllis' hair. It consisted of a mixture of equal amounts of sage tea and whiskey. To that "cocktail," a dash of quinine was added and stirred in. The concoction was then painted onto the scalp at least twice a day. It didn't work.

**Homer at age 18 in Peno Bottom, Oklahoma**

To help her little sister as best she could, Bon fashioned a way to tie a scarf around Phyllis' head that was secure, somewhat fashionable, and allowed the hair around her ears to show. Eventually, Phyllis was given a wig made of human hair that allowed her to regain a bit of her confidence. As she got older and married, she added a number of high-quality wigs to her collection, but scarves tied in the way Bon had come up with were all she wore during her leisure time for the remainder of her life.

For the next few years, the Eubanks kids left home one at a time as they grew up. The younger Eubanks kids, those who were products of Papa's and T. Lou's marriage and the children Papa's second wife brought into the marriage, were still at home and kept the youthful feel alive in the tired old farmhouse. Papa's two late-in-life children were Lola Dean and Robert, Jr. They fit right in with the older Eubanks kids and seemed to worship their older siblings.

Bon packed her belongings in two paper sacks and traveled from Fort Smith to Marshall on the bus. She hadn't been there long before Phyllis showed up in Marshall and moved in with her older siblings. They promptly enrolled her in school, and when she finished high school a few years later, they sent her to live with Ab in Lubbock and enrolled her in Texas Tech.

Paul had found work in Tulsa in the oil industry. While there, he married Wilma Hefly and they, too, headed for Texas. Homer left Oklahoma for Marshall when he was 20 and sunk roots there that only deepened throughout his life.

Homer matured into a ruggedly handsome man with broad shoulders, long sinewy arms, and fists that belonged on a much larger man. His air of confidence and common sense enabled him to make friends–men and women–easily. His reputation as a tough guy didn't take long to rear itself in Marshall.

The incident that fueled it occurred innocently enough when Homer applied for his first job in Marshall, that of an ice delivery wagon driver for Marshall Ice Company. Homer was hired on the spot and told to show up early the next morning to get his team of horses and wagon. Eager to make a good impression, the 20-year-old was the first to report for duty the next morning. The foreman told him to go to the barn and pick out his animals, hook them up to a wagon, and wait for his route instructions at the dock. Having grown up around work horses, mules, and wagons, Homer picked what he thought to be the best team. As he and his team stood below the loading dock, other drivers soon came and hooked up their teams. They joined Homer at the foot of the dock. He noticed a couple of the men looked his team over and followed their inspections with looks at Homer with large eyes that bespoke alarm. He soon found out why they had given him the looks of concern.

**Homer at the Sabine River, near Marshall, Texas**

A large, barrel-chested man walked across the dock and stopped in front of Homer, glared down at him, and in a stern and threatening voice, told Homer he had chosen the wrong team for his wagon. He followed that up by telling the young man that he had selected his personal team and that Homer needed to move "his" mules over to his wagon or get his ass kicked all the way around the town square. Homer slowly climbed the stairs onto the dock and ambled toward the intimidating man. He softly told the big man that the boss had told him to take his pick of the mules and he had done just that. By this time, the other drivers and the foreman had gathered at the foot of the dock to watch the action.

Though wide at the shoulders, long armed, and big fisted, Homer was only 5'10" tall and weighed about 165 pounds. The only things intimidating about him were his quiet confidence and piercing eyes. The big man outweighed Homer by at least 50 pounds, and it was obvious that he was used to getting his way at the Marshall Ice Company. His name was Brady Waggert and, apparently, Waggert was known as maybe the toughest guy in Marshall, if not all of East Texas. He had left bumps, bruises, and scars all over the Piney Woods. Homer did not know Waggert, nor had he heard of his reputation as a man to steer clear of.

As Homer slowly approached the big man, those watching may have admired the new guy's courage, but they feared for his safety. Brady was somewhat taken aback by the boldness of the young man but showed no fear at all. In-

Homer at the Gulf Station he managed in Marshall, Texas, 1932. Note the pistol in his belt

stead, he braced his stance and offered a wry grin to Homer. Homer watched the bully's eyes closely as he told the bigger man he liked the team he had chosen and planned to keep them. As the big man narrowed his eyes and pulled his right arm back for a punch, Homer landed three blows in his face before Brady could unload a strike. Each blow had power and snapped the big man's head back sharply. The fight was over at that point, but Brady didn't fully realize it. He stumbled toward Homer trying to grab him, but the speedy 20-year-old sidestepped his advance and delivered a body-jarring blow to the aggressor's left ear. Waggert flailed aimlessly in the air as Homer finished the job with a left-right combination that dropped the big man to the floor of the dock. He was out. The shocked throng of workers rushed up to Homer and tried to take in what they had just seen. Their disbelief was etched on their faces, and a murmur of admiration for the young battler was pervasive. It seems Waggert had bullied and persecuted all of his co-workers in the past and they had longed for the day when someone would put him down. That day had arrived.

Homer's reputation for the beatdown he had given to the bully, Brady Waggert, spread through Marshall rapidly, and the young man from Peno Bottom rode his newfound fame into the social structure of the young Marshallites. Over the next couple of years, he and his new best friend, Gibby Morrison, became quite popular on the party circuit. The fun-loving duo enjoyed the wild side of life and became the go-to guys for those looking for fun. Homer and Gibby took over the operations of a gasoline station and did well enough to co-buy a new yellow Stutz Bearcat. The Stutz became well-known around town as the car either going to a party or the car coming from a party. Its notoriety got a real boost one Saturday night when it drove down Washington Street, the city's main business street, with a topless woman perched on its hood posed as a hood ornament. After causing quite a stir, the boys were pulled over by the police. Homer and Gibby received citations for indecency while the buxom blonde only received a blanket with which to cover up.

Even though Homer had very few skirmishes after his beating of the town bully, his fame for being tough lived on. In fact, one day while he was working at the station, he was approached by a man in a three-piece suit and offered an unusual job. The man, a Mr. Landrum, was an official of a national chemical company that had a large distribution warehouse and railroad yard located in Marshall. They had 26 employees, a general manager, and two foremen: one for the warehouse crew and one for the yard crew. Mr. Landrum told Homer that his firm wanted to hire him to fire the yard foreman. He went on to explain that previous efforts to terminate the man had failed and, since everyone was afraid of the man, they needed Homer to do the firing. They knew of Homer's fight at the icehouse and figured he could handle the situation if the foreman refused to be fired. Mr. Landrum offered Homer $100 if he could pull off the job, an exorbitant amount of money at that time.

Homer accepted the job and received a briefing from Landrum and Clarence Weeks, the general manager. It was decided that on payday, Homer would take the foreman his check and tell him he was fired and had to clear off the site. When payday rolled around, Homer set out to do his job by seeking out the foreman who was in the yard. Landrum and Weeks stepped out into the yard to watch what was about to transpire. Homer found his target leaning against a boxcar and handed him his check. When he told him he was fired and had to clear out, the burly, red-faced man did not respond. He simply turned as though to walk away and then quickly spun around with a right hook that caught Homer on the chin and caused him to stagger several steps backwards. Homer was trying to shake off the effects of the hard right as the man stepped forward and continued his attack. Homer was clearly dazed and was trying to just fend off the flurry of fists while he gathered himself and found the strength to fight back. Homer caught a break when the foreman launched a roundhouse right at Homer's head. The wobbly young man managed to duck the incoming missile causing it to make solid contact with the steel side of the nearby boxcar. The pain from hitting the rail car slowed the foreman long enough for

Homer, age 22

Homer to get his legs back and launch his counterattack. A knock-down, drag-out fist fight followed, with each man scoring damaging blows. Homer finally k.o.'d the foreman, but he always wondered whether he could've whipped the guy if the brawler hadn't damaged his right hand with his errant right cross. He vowed that from that day on he would never allow himself to be surprised by an unexpected first punch.

A few weeks after he had returned to the station, Borden Milk's local manager offered Homer a job collecting past-due debts from commercial customers who were seriously in arrears. Homer was to be paid a salary and a percentage of anything he collected. With Gibby's blessing, he took the Borden's offer and set about collecting the delinquent accounts. Homer knew most of the debtors and was able to work out debt repayment plans with most of them. Despite his toughness, Homer had an easy smile and an attractive personality that helped him in his new job. His success rate was high and Borden's was elated with his success, but trouble with one of the bad-debt boys was about to take center stage.

Homer pulled up to the small gas station that sat across West Houston Street from Marshall High School, grabbed the owner's past-due bill, and walked up the three small concrete steps into the station's office intent on collecting some, if not all, of the money the owner owed. The office was small. It had a small wooden desk, two chairs, and a stand-up cooler with see-through glass doors that held a few soft drinks, three quarts of milk, and a handful of sandwiches wrapped in brown butcher paper. The man sitting at the desk, Donald Barstow, offered a warm welcome and an offer to help Homer. Homer sat in one of the chairs, showed the man the past due bill and explained the options open to the station owner. Barstow remained calm and cordial as he listened and looked over the bills. He then pulled his wallet out of his back pocket and counted out the full amount of the debt. He gave the money to Homer, who, in turn, gave the man a receipt for the payment. Both men rose from their chairs and shook hands as Barstow came from behind his desk.

Homer then turned and started down the three steps when all hell broke out. Barstow hit Homer on the top of his head with a monkey wrench. He repeated the assault each time Homer took a step down. The three blows from the wrench caused Homer to wobble noticeably, but he never went down. It was clear to the wounded collector that Barstow was momentarily confused by Homer's failure to go down from the blows. His indecision about whether to continue his attack or to run for cover gave Homer time to shake the cobwebs from his brain and move toward the wrench-wielding man. He grabbed the right wrist of Barstow, which still held the wrench, and delivered a jaw-shattering right-hand punch that caused the man to wilt as though someone had let all of the air out of him. Homer then sat down on the steps next to the unconscious Barstow and allowed his head to quit throbbing.

Before Homer had fully recovered, a Marshall Police car wheeled into the station's driveway with sirens and red light going full bore. With gun drawn, the policeman cautiously approached the two battered men. When he recognized Homer, he re-holstered his pistol and, after helping Bartow to a seated position, started his interview of the two warriors. As Barstow slowly came back to life, Homer gave his account of what had transpired. Barstow, who was still groggy, disputed Homer's account and fixed all of the blame on the Borden's man. The policeman was about to haul both men to the station when a young math teacher from the high school walked over to the gas station and quickly told the policeman she had witnessed the entire drama. Her name was Gussie Roughton, and she had been standing on the school campus just across Houston Street from the station. She had seen the two men shake hands and had seen Barstow attack Homer from behind with the monkey wrench. Her story matched Homer's, so the policeman told him he could go. He thanked Miss Gussie for coming forward and then loaded Barstow in his car for his trip to jail.

Homer and Gibby sold their station for a nice profit a few months after his stint as Borden's debt collector. They kept their Stutz Bearcat and their partying ways but, for the most part, Homer's fighting days were over. He had been fighting his whole life, and he had decided enough was enough. He suffered regularly with severe headaches, probably the result of having taken many blows to the head. The railroad bull's nightstick to the head and the resultant blow he took to the head when thrown from the train probably did damage that never healed. Three blows from a monkey wrench surely only exacerbated his injuries. Homer's headaches weren't ever mollified by the large quantities of alcohol he consumed on a regular basis. The headaches and his struggles to control his alcohol intake were conditions that clouded parts of his life for the rest of his days.

## The Courtship of Zelma Chance

Gibby and Homer had been invited to attend an off-campus party being hosted by a sorority from the College of Marshall. Never ones to pass up a good party, the boys accepted and made the scene at the Sabine River site just off the Henderson Highway the girls had chosen for their party. Not long after the party had begun, Homer caught sight of a co-ed who was the most beautiful woman he had ever seen. He was instantly smitten, and he just couldn't take his eyes off of the tall, willowy girl with the raven black hair.

She seemed to be spending most of her time with a fun-loving character by the name of Glenn Link. Homer was unsure about the girl's relationship with Mr. Link, so he introduced himself to Glenn and asked if he and the pretty girl were dating. Glenn just laughed and told Homer they had grown up together in New Boston, Texas, and were like brother and sister. He then offered to introduce Homer to his "sister" and Homer quickly accepted the offer. It was then and there that Homer met the love of his life, Zelma Cecilia Chance. That introduction started a lifelong friendship between Homer and Glenn and a much more important relationship between Homer and the beautiful young co-ed.

Homer and Gibby returned to their fun-loving lifestyle after the college sorority party in the Sabine River bottom off the Henderson Highway, but Gibby could tell Homer's heart wasn't in the effort. Homer had been branded with a large "Z" on his brain, and that "Z" stood for Zelma.

Zelma, called Zee by Homer and most of her friends, was an 18-year-old college freshman from New Boston, Texas, a town of about 1,000 people in 1930. Tucked away in Northeast Texas, New Boston lies 21 miles west of Texarkana and about eight miles south of the Red River.

It was timber country and Zelma's father, Lee, was in the timber business. He owned a sawmill and several hundred acres of timber land known as the Red River Farm.

Lee was also a well-known high stakes gambler who participated in poker games of several days in duration that featured prominent gamblers from his native Chicago, Milwaukee, St. Louis, and Kansas City. When the gamblers gathered at the Chance house for their game, Zelma and her two older sisters, Mary and Maudie, served the gamblers their food and kept the ash trays emptied and the poker room clean throughout the multi-day game. When one of the gamblers needed a rest, he would retire to a bedroom with three single beds in it for an hour or two of shuteye. The game never stopped during these respites. When the game was finally over, Zelma, Mary and Maudie were handsomely tipped by each of the visiting gamblers, sometimes getting $50 to $100 from each of their dad's friends.

Unlike Homer, Zelma had grown up in comfort, causing many of their friends to consider them an unusual pairing. Money wasn't the only factor that separated the young lovers. Her genteel beauty was in stark contrast to his rugged good looks. She was educated. He wasn't. She played tennis, badminton, canasta, and bridge. He didn't. She lived a moderate, if not controlled, life. He didn't.

Despite their differences, Homer pursued a relationship with the young beauty, and the two began dating. About the same time, Gibby fell madly in love with a girl named Nora, whom he eventually married, so the two couples formed a friendship that lasted throughout their lives.

The onset of the Great Depression caused the boys to sell their Stutz Bearcat and relinquish management of the service station they had successfully run for several years. America was on its heels, still reeling from the devastation of the war in Europe and still in the shadow of the influenza pandemic that killed millions throughout the world.

The massive sell-off of stocks in 1929 signaled a loss of faith in the U.S. economy that lasted ten long years, during which one-half of the world's banks closed and unemployment stayed around 25%. The Great Depression spared few from its devastation, and brought intense hardship to most people, especially those with few resources. Shortly after the Depression had settled in and established itself as a condition for which there was no easy fix, a drought plagued much of the nation's prairie land and caused countless acres of wheat and other commodities to dry up and yield their roots to the relentless winds that swept through most of Western Oklahoma, a large chunk of West Texas and its panhandle, and parts of Kansas and Colorado. The drought raged unabated from 1930 to 1936 and the affected area was peppered relentlessly by ruthless dust storms and high winds that blew unchecked by vegetation that had died of thirst. It was the Dust Bowl and, during its reign of tragedy, more than 7,000 people died of what became known as "dust pneumonia." The financial hardship Dust Bowl families endured added considerably to the severity of the Depression.

It was hard for people to find happiness at this time in America with these economic monsters circling their lives like impatient vultures, but Homer and Zelma did. Their love for each other propelled them over and through the obstacles that were derailing so many folks. Homer found work as a milkman with Borden's and Zelma continued her education at the College of Marshall.

Homer's oldest sister, Vina, and her husband, Lee, opened their home on Alamo Street in Marshall to her siblings and took over the responsibilities of getting all of them through the hard times. She managed their collective monies and was able to stretch their incomes enough to see them through the Depression without having to stand in soup lines. Throughout her life, Vina was always strong enough to steer her loved ones through troubled waters. Her brothers and sisters were in awe of her strength. They also were afraid to ever challenge her.

Homer and Zelma were deeply in love with each other, and Vina soon embraced Zelma as a member of the Eubanks family.

## Three Marks on a Milk Bottle

With a little finagling, Homer was able to get his milk route amended to include Zelma's sorority house on the campus of the College of Marshall. His delivery to the kitchen at the Zeta Mu Epsilon sorority house was through the back door and into the kitchen. It was handled early in the morning before any of the social sisters were astir.

At that time, milk was delivered in glass quart-sized bottles, each of which was topped by a cardboard disk that had to be removed before the milk could be served. Homer soon began marking each of the paper lids with three vertical lines drawn in ink, underscored by three horizontal lines. He knew that when Zelma came down for breakfast, she would see the three marks on her milk bottle and know that he was thinking of her and loved her. The three marks, which stood for the three words "I love you," quickly became the way the young lovers signed all their correspondence. They soon expanded the use of the three marks to encompass the way they waved at each other. Their waves to each other became the waving of three fingers as just another way of demonstrating their love for each other.

Ultimately, their personal method of intimately communicating with each other was expanded to include the use of three sharp whistles when they wanted to get their partner's attention across the room or in a crowd. All three private ways of saying "I love you" stuck with the couple throughout their lives and were even passed down to their three sons. Not surprisingly, Homer's and Zelma's sons continued the three-mark tradition through their courtships, into their marriages, and passed it on to their children, their children's children, and to their great grandchildren. The three-marks are now being used by the fifth generation of Eubankses to express their love uniquely to family members.

The three-mark method of reminding a loved one of your love for them has taken on many other forms through the generations of Homer's and Zelma's offspring. Many pieces of jewelry exchanged within the Eubanks family have been engraved with the three marks. The three marks are now carved into the headstones marking the graves of family members. When Homer and Zelma's middle son, Robert, bought a small farm in Mississippi, he promptly named it Three Whistles Farm. The symbol of family love has been baked into china and painted subtly into commissioned oil paintings and pieces of pottery. Its many uses by family members to record their love for one another proudly but in a confidential manner has become a heartfelt source of pride for the entire Eubanks family. The waving of the three fingers to a loved one, the sound of the three whistles to a loved one, and the signing of letters and notes from one loved one to another, communicated more than love. They served to tell the recipient "well done" or "I'm with you" also. The cumulative effect of Eubanks children growing up in a family environment that expressed itself in this manner no doubt served to wrap the children in a comfortable blanket of caring that kept them from ever wondering if they were loved. They also remind later generations of the love that united Homer and Zelma in the early 1930s. Homer surely never would have dreamed that his making those three marks on his Zee's milk bottle lid would lead to a family tradition that spread the love that he felt for Zelma so early-on in their relationship.

**Zelma with her sorority sisters at College at Marshall (top row, fourth from the left)**

## The Wrong Homer Eubanks

The mule barn in Jefferson, Texas was the undisputed best mule barn in all of East Texas and Western Louisiana. Farmers from throughout the region in need of a mule usually found their way to the Jefferson mule barn. It had the largest selection of mules, the healthiest mules, and the biggest mules. It was the mule supermarket. Because of its fame, the mule barn was also a tourist attraction that drew countless visitors to Jefferson.

On auction days, mule buyers and traders filled virtually all of the hotel and boarding house rooms in Jefferson and in Marshall, which was only thirteen miles from Jefferson. Jefferson's historic and majestic Excelsior Hotel was the center of the action that accompanied the mule auctions because the wealthiest buyers and sellers stayed at the luxury hotel. The Excelsior, which opened in the 1850s, claimed Ulysses S. Grant, Oscar Wilde, and Rutherford B. Hayes among its famous customers. Its elegance and noted customers brought fame to the grand old hotel, but it was the mule auctions that brought it to life. The barn and its auction ring were only one block from downtown Jefferson, so all of downtown was a beehive of activity on sale days.

Homer had been raised on working farms and had worked mules countless hours as a boy and young man. In doing so, he had developed a solid admiration for mules and their strength, durability, and independence. He had learned that if a plowing mule needed a break, he would just stop, and all of the prodding and cussing on earth couldn't cajole him into action. The hardheaded rascal would resume plowing when he was good and ready; not a minute before. Homer also learned that when there was a fresh-cut stump in a mule's sight, the mule would frequently make a beeline for it, dragging plow and the guy doing the plowing along for the ride. The mule would then suck on the fresh stump's edges until it had its fill of whatever it was extracting. Stump-sucking mules could really slow down a day of row plowing. Veteran mule folks thought stump-sucking was the result of a mule's deficiency in a certain vitamin.

Suffice it say, Homer loved mules, and he seldom missed a Jefferson mule auction. He didn't buy or sell mules, he just loved to see them and watch the auction action. It was a sale day that brought Homer to Jefferson on Friday, the first day of the two-day sale.

After a hearty breakfast at a small café on Austin Street in downtown Jefferson, Homer was walking toward the mule barn when, all at once, two men grabbed him by the arms and threw him up against the display window at Joseph's Apparel and Dry Goods store. In shock, Homer tried to spin around to see who his attackers were, but as he tried to twist free of the men's grips, one of them hit him on the back of his head with what he later learned was a nine and one-half inch slap jack, a leather device that had a leather bulb on its end filled with lead shot. It put Homer out.

When he woke up, he found himself in a cell in the basement of the Marion County Courthouse. When the jailer, a sheriff's deputy, heard Homer stirring, he brought the woozy young man a glass of water. He then told Homer that he and the high sheriff had arrested him on an outstanding warrant and that the sheriff was the one who hit him with the slap jack. When he asked to speak to the sheriff, Homer was informed that the sheriff was in Dallas for the weekend and would be back on Monday. Until then, he would have to stay in jail. Homer learned from the deputy that the warrant had been sworn out by a woman named Verna Mattox, who lived in the Marion County unincorporated community of Potter's Point. She claimed that Homer Eubanks had robbed her and stolen her car while she slept. Homer had never heard of the lady, nor had he robbed anyone or stolen a car. The deputy didn't buy Homer's denial of guilt and reminded his jailbird that the name "Homer Eubanks" wasn't exactly a common name. Even Homer had to agree with the jailer's logic.

Sheriff Mason Blackburn showed up at the jail at 7 a.m. Monday morning, filled his mug with coffee, and pulled up a chair next to Homer's cell. Homer's request for a cup of the strong-smelling coffee was refused, but the sheriff said he could have some with his breakfast later that morning. Blackburn repeated the information from the warrant issued by Judge Shivers and said that Homer would appear before the judge at 3 o'clock that afternoon.

Homer listened to the sheriff calmly and then received the lawman's okay to give his version of the story. After explaining that he had never heard of Verna Mattox, had never robbed anyone or stolen a car, he suggested that the sheriff bring Ms. Mattox in to see if he was, in fact, the fellow who had wronged her. After sipping on his coffee, he nodded and instructed his deputy to pick up Miss Verna and bring her in for an identification.

While waiting on his deputy's return, the sheriff and Homer continued to discuss the situation. Homer told the sheriff he lived in Marshall and gave him names of respected Marshallites who would vouch for his character and good citizenship. The sheriff decided making a few calls to Marshall to check on Eubanks might be good policing. After having done so, he wandered back to Homer's cell and told him he checked out to be a good and trustworthy man. He didn't tell Homer that he had also been advised by those he spoke to not to mistreat Homer, as he was quite capable of exacting revenge. The good reports, and, perhaps, the not-so-subtle threats that Homer was not to be trifled with, clearly softened the sheriff's disposition toward Homer, and he asked Homer if he still wanted that cup of coffee. Homer nodded yes and was promptly served by the now somewhat confounded sheriff. Blackburn's remaining skepticism came through when he, almost jokingly, said that too much alcohol could surely make a man do stupid things. Homer didn't bite on the statement. He just kept sipping his jailhouse coffee.

When the deputy and Miss Verna showed up about ten minutes later, the affable Homer had Sheriff Blackburn laughing uncontrollably, and the two of them seemed as though they were longtime pals. After noticing that his deputy and Miss Verna had arrived, Blackburn slowly stood, wiped the laughter tears from his eyes, rearranged his sidearm to its proper place on his hip and asked Miss Verna to step in front of the cell for an identification of the man who had robbed her.

The still-angry Verna Mattox stared in at Homer Eubanks and, with her hands firmly planted on her generous hips, told Sheriff Blackburn the man he had in jail was not Homer Eubanks. Based on her adamancy and after thinking it through, the sheriff had Homer's cell door opened and the four of them sat in a circle in the office while the sheriff tried to figure out what the hell was going on.

It turns out that Verna had been keeping company with a man named Homer Eubanks from Atlanta, Texas, a small town located between Jefferson and Texarkana. Her Homer was considerably older than this Homer. On the night of the robbery and car theft, Verna and her Homer had over-imbibed and argued until she passed out. Apparently, while she was sleeping it off, the Homer from Atlanta stole her blind and drove off in her car. Case closed. The wrong Homer Eubanks had been clubbed over the head and spent three nights in the Marion County jail for a crime he didn't commit. It was good news for Homer, but an oh hell moment for the Marion County sheriff.

**Epilogue:** There were no reparations for the injustice Homer had received; just a very nervous apology and two packets of Goody's headache powder for the headache from which he'd suffered for the past three days. When Homer left the jail, Blackburn couldn't help but wonder if Homer would exact revenge for the wrongful arrest and beating he had suffered. The words about Homer's toughness he had heard from the Marshall folks he had talked to just kept echoing in his head.

Homer never even got to see the mules, which was his entire reason for being in Jefferson. He would continue to love mules. Jefferson? Not so much. The criminal Homer Eubanks from Atlanta, Texas was captured, convicted, and served twelve months in the Huntsville State Prison. When he was released from prison, he and Verna re-kindled their romance. They moved to Marshall and immediately started running up bad debts. Debt collectors often confused the two Homer Eubankses, causing much embarrassment and trouble to Homer and Zelma who had married and started their family. In frustration, Homer sought out and found the second Homer in Marshall and, in the most emphatic way possible, suggested Marshall wasn't big enough for two Homer Eubankses. The intimidation worked and Homer and Verna moved to Mineral Wells, Texas. Problem solved.

## Homer and Zee Sink Their Roots

After their marriage in 1932, Homer and Zee moved into a small second story apartment in an old Victorian house on Marshall's West Houston Street. Zelma, or Zee, as Homer called her, had finished the two years of college required for a teaching certificate, and got a job teaching elementary school. The new bride was beautiful, happy, intelligent, at home in the classroom, and completely lost in the kitchen. Her mother, Josephine, had never taught her how to cook. In fact, Zee and her sisters had been raised in a home with a maid who also prepared all of their meals.

Homer, who had been a self-sufficient bachelor for some time, accepted the challenge of teaching Zee how to cook. He began by teaching her how to make coffee. His way of doing so involved throwing away the insides of the coffee pot, putting the water and coffee in the pot and boiling it. He called it creek bottom coffee, and it became the only way the couple made their coffee throughout their marriage. He also showed her that if you put eggshells in the boiling pot, the coffee grounds would settle to the bottom of the pot, leaving the coffee grounds-free for drinking He then focused on teaching her how to make several kinds of gravy. Once he had taken care of showing her the ropes about making coffee and gravy, his priorities had been met and the rest came easy.

While Zelma brought style, grace, and gentility to the marriage, Homer contributed energy, unbridled optimism, and a passion for life. She was timid. He was confident. She was demure. He was bold. Her face was soft and white. His was rugged, scarred, and tanned. Without a doubt, Homer brought some rough edges into their marriage, ones Zelma helped to smooth off through the years.

Homer, who was five years older than Zelma, had been shaped by the many challenges he had overcome in his life. He had been a fighter–both literally and figuratively–since he was a young boy. When he and his best friend, Gibby, had become mainstays on the party scene in Marshall, Homer became quite attached to alcohol. In fact, the fondness he developed for it at that time, reared its head off and on throughout his life. He never drank every day, but, when he did drink, he tended to drink all day.

Despite what he lacked in formal education, the degree he earned from the school of hard knocks gave Homer strong coping skills and an indisputable amount of common sense. His ability to fit comfortably into any situation and any mixture of people always amazed Zee, and her reliance on Homer's adaptability and leadership gave her coattails on which to ride into many situations that were new to her. She kept Homer grounded and gave him a loving home base that served him well.

The many fights in which he had taken part and the many blows he had taken to his head from fists, wrenches, clubs, and slap jacks caused Homer to suffer from intense headaches throughout his life that were resistant to analgesics and other pain relievers. Doctors were at a loss as to how to help him. He just had to suffer through them, and some of them lasted up to twenty-four hours. When one of the headaches took hold of him, Homer's eyes turned bright red, and he paced countless hours, as rest of any kind was impossible. The minute one of his headaches had run its course, Homer instantly sprang back and resumed his charge through life. When lucky, he might go several weeks in a row without a headache.

The marriage of Homer and Zelma clearly gave some validity to the old axiom that opposites attract. Many observers felt as though their love was reminiscent of the fairy tale that was written in 1740, *Beauty and the Beast*. While Homer displayed a confident bravado as he met life's challenges, it was Zelma that kept the fierceness that bounced around inside Homer's chest contained. In jest, but embodying more truth than fiction, Homer once told a group of his friends, "I am the boss of my family, and I have Zee's permission to say so."

Soon after their marriage, Zelma became pregnant. She was able to finish her first–and last–year of teaching shortly before she gave birth to their first son, whom they named Homer Alvin Eubanks, Jr. The year was 1933, and the Great Depression was at its point of greatest impact, with more than twenty per cent of the nation's population unemployed.

Because building had virtually stopped in America, Zelma's Mother and Dad had sold their sawmill and land in New Boston and moved to Marshall, where Lee became the top timber estimator for Key Industries, the largest timber and lumber operation in East Texas. It was said that Lee Chance could walk through a field of timber and estimate its wood yield within a few board feet. When it was time for Zee to give birth, she went to her parents' house to do so. This enabled her mother to take care of her during and after the birth.

The sorry state of economic affairs in the country was no match for Homer's zeal for his little family and their future. He, Zee, and their new son moved to a larger home in Marshall's East End. Homer had been in Marshall long enough to establish his reputation as a man of high energy and strong character. Because of his good reputation, he never went without a job during the Depression.

Homer and his small family, like most others during the bleak years, struggled financially and learned to live with less. They, again, like most others, adjusted to moderation—moderation in everything but the love they shared. It was healthy and grew each day of their union.

In 1936, Zelma gave birth to another son. He was named Robert Lee, taking the first names of his two grandfathers. He, like his older brother, was born at his grandparents' home with the Marshall medical fixture, Dr. Galen Eads, handling the delivery.

While the Depression showed signs of lessening its stranglehold on America's economy, finances were still tight for most Americans in 1936. Homer and Zee were still keeping their heads above water, but prosperity was a distant dream throughout the 1930s. Most Americans stood on shaky legs, still reeling from the harsh body blows they had sustained from the Depression, droughts, Hitler's war in Europe, and other maladies that plagued that decade.

London's Guardian Newspaper called the 1930s "humanity's darkest, bloodiest hour...a decade haunted by mass poverty and violent extremism." Although the War had not yet been joined by the United States, it cast an ominous shadow over America that kept its citizens on edge. Clearly, the 1930s was a decade bruised, battered, and scarred by multiple hardships and evils.

East Texas and its population received another bone-jarring jolt on March 13, 1937, at 3:17 in the afternoon, when a natural gas explosion ripped through the junior and senior high school building of New London, Texas. The blast killed more than 300 students and teachers and flattened buildings throughout the town of 1,200 residents. The Consolidated London School of New London had 594 students and forty teachers present at the time of the explosion, which was heard and felt as far as forty miles away. It occurred just thirteen minutes before the bell rang that would dismiss everyone in the building.

New London was right in the middle of the mammoth and legendary East Texas Oil Field, twenty-four miles southeast of Tyler. There were approximately ten thousand producing oil wells in New London at the time, with eleven of those being on the school ground.

At the time of the tragedy, natural gas had no odor, so the explosion came with no warning. Within weeks of that devastating event, the Texas Legislature passed a law requiring that natural gas be odorized. From that point on, natural gas has been infused with the chemical mercaptan, giving it the distinctive smell of rotten eggs. A German scientist had infused natural gas with ethyl mercaptan in the 1880s, but the practice did not become mandatory until the New London explosion.

Following the school blast, political, religious, and business leaders from throughout the world flooded New London with telegrams and letters of condolence. Adolf Hitler was among those letter writers.

Homer's sister, Bonnie Eubanks Kash of Marshall, Texas, kept a scrapbook of the many articles and photographs that appeared

Homer with sisters Bon (left) and Phyllis (right)

detailing the explosion and its heartbreaking aftermath. Her scrapbook, which now belongs to the New London Museum, also included many notes she wrote chronicling the impressions she formed as a participant in the massive clean-up effort.

Bonnie's journal documented the following account of Homer's and Zelma's rescue efforts following the explosion. She wrote, "Homer and Zelma were on the scene within two hours after it happened, and Homer helped in the rescue and recovery work for most all night. (He) saw some terrible sights which left him nervous and nauseated for days. Homer, Jr. was three and one-half at the time and he sat on a fire truck with the firemen and took it all in."

Bonnie described volunteers walking through town looking for bodies and body parts. She described the scene as "gruesome and sad" and said the experience left permanent scars on the hearts of all who witnessed the scene.

Homer's generation seemed to live next door to tragedy. The Spanish Flu, the Dust Bowl, World War I, and the Great Depression combined forces to beat the hell out of that generation. Little did they know, World War II was just around the corner. After so much adversity, Homer and his generation mustered their resilience and rebuilt after each of those near-fatal incidents in history.

As is always the case, time and life marched onward and put the past in the rearview mirror. Homer had a good job with Borden's, but he felt underchallenged and ached for a business of his own.

Things began to change one day in late 1937 when Homer was walking on the eastern edge of Downtown Marshall and noticed a "for rent" sign on a large commercial space on the Northeast corner of Austin and Bolivar Streets. Never one to sit on his hands, Homer borrowed the telephone at the Hub Shoe Store, which was two doors down from the vacant building, to call Zee and tell her to grab the boys and hustle on downtown to see what he had found.

When Zee and the boys had completed their four-block walk to downtown, she spotted Homer excitedly pacing up and down in front of a vacant building. When he saw them heading his way, he excitedly rushed to them and met them half a block away. He then ushered them up to the large plate glass window of the vacant building and told them to look into the building and tell him what they saw. The four-year-old Homer, Jr. said he saw dust. One year-old Robert was too young to answer or even understand the question, and Zee looked at her husband with a look that perfectly portrayed her mixture of curiosity, nervousness, and excitement.

Homer draped his arms on Zee's shoulders and said, "Zee, you are looking at the soon-to-be Eubanks Quality Food Store." With that pronouncement, Homer involved himself in a flurry of high-speed activity that included negotiating a lease with the Suddoth Family that owned the building, arranging equipment leasing and financing, and getting commitments from suppliers. In record time, Homer tied up all of his loose ends and opened for business.

Eubanks Quality Foods quickly built a loyal following and broke into the profit column in relatively short order. Homer ran the store and Zelma kept the books and paid the bills. Their economic outlook was looking rosy and business continued to grow right up until Eubanks Quality Foods received a crippling blow.

Homer had operated his store on a three-year lease with Mr. Suddoth and he fully planned–and expected–to renew for at least another three years, as he and his young family were enjoying a taste of success that allowed them to think that success was achievable. Mr. Suddoth now had other plans for his building, plans that would leave Eubanks Quality Foods without a home. Mr. Suddoth, an electrician by trade, had decided that he and his son would open Suddoth Electric and Lighting Fixtures in the space. He realized his plans created major hardships for Homer, so he gave Homer a six-month extension on his lease, hoping it would give the young grocer time to find a new space.

Homer was unable to find a suitable space, but he did find a vacant lot he thought was ideally located for a new building for Eubanks Quality Foods. It was on the Southeast corner of East Houston and Alamo Streets. Homer made a down payment on the lot and set about trying to secure financing for his new building.

Early on, he called on his friend S. E. Wood, Sr., a well-respected entrepreneur, to seek his counsel. Wood, who had been a customer of Homer's, listened to Homer's plans and his needs and then, to Homer's amazement, he told Homer he would build the building for him and finance the entire venture. Wood told Homer he would need some building plans before he could begin construction, so Homer promised he would get right on it and excused himself.

Three hours later, Homer returned to Mr. Wood's office and it was his turn to amaze his financier. He proceeded to place a set of hand-drawn plans on Wood's desk. While the drawings were rather crude and, in fact, were sketched on the front and back of a brown paper sack, they included details such as electrical outlets, plumbing specifics, lighting needs, loading dock heights, and color specs. Wood looked them over and asked questions for about twenty minutes. He then told Homer he could build from the plans and pronounced the project a "go." Their deal was consummated with a handshake. It was perhaps a sign of the times that a written contact was not needed. An agreement among honorable men sealed with a handshake was good enough.

Construction on the new store began in late 1939. Eubanks Quality Foods was about to get a new home.

## Open for Business

In the autumn of 1940, a full-page advertisement in the *Marshall News Messenger* announced that Eubanks Quality Foods was open for business in its new location on the corner of East Houston and Alamo. It featured a large photograph of the store's new building and smiling mugshots of Homer, L. V. O'Bannon, Homer's nephew and new partner, and Sidney Moon, the store's delivery man and all-around helper. As was the custom in 1940, other Marshall merchants ran congratulatory and good luck ads to support Homer's and L.V.'s new venture.

The store got off to a good start and business was brisk. While the lovable, good-spirited, L.V., who was Homer's oldest sister Vina's son, failed miserably at working in the store, his occasional visits kept the mood fun and light. He made no bones about the fact that he just wasn't cut out for the grocery business. He soon gave his Uncle Homer (whom he called Unca Homa) his share of the business back and went into the real estate business. By doing so, he maximized his control of how he spent his time and energy. While somewhat successful in the real estate business, he still managed to spend much of his time socializing and golfing at Marshall Lakeside Country Club. He would still make frequent cameo appearances at the store, mainly because Homer was his best drinking buddy, and the two men were as close as fleas on a hound's back. The two of them loved each other very much, but it became abundantly clear that the time they spent together brought out and magnified each other's weaknesses.

Cars and trucks clearly owned the streets and highways in the early 1940s, but there were still enough horse or mule-drawn wagons around rural East Texas to remind everyone of their rural roots in the not-so-distant past. The wagons evoked one of two reactions as the mules that pulled them clopped their way through the paved streets of Marshall. Some folks paused and admired their wagon-afforded glimpses into the past, while others honked or yelled at these vestiges because they were slowing the traffic to a crawl.

One wagon that was a fixture around Marshall was a mule-drawn wagon driven by an aged pig farmer named Landy. Landy's wagon had wooden side rails on it so the six large barrels he hauled around wouldn't fall out of the wagon. The farmer's regular route took him to all of the grocery stores and cafes in town so he could pick up spoiled and uneaten foods to take to his pigs. Most of the grocers and café owners knew Landy's pick-up schedule and put stuff aside for him to load into his barrels. Eubanks Quality Foods was near the end of Landy's route, so by the time he got there, his barrels were usually pretty full. They also stunk to high heavens and attracted countless swarms of flies and a number of dogs, cats, and birds seduced by the aroma and prospects of dining on spillage. The birds generally perched on the sides of the barrels, while the dogs and cats trailed along behind the wagon praying for slop spills.

Late one afternoon, Landy pulled up to the rear of Homer's store to make his pick-up and was spotted by Homer and L.V., who were into the happy stage of an afternoon of drinking. Homer and L.V. hatched a plan that, once carried out, would live in humorous infamy for years to come. The businessmen gave Landy five dollars and an R.C. Cola in exchange for the use of his wagon for a short while.

As the tipsy men climbed onto the wagon's seat, Homer stood and took the reins and L.V. stood at his uncle's side laughing and hollering. It should be noted that L.V. had a very loud and clear voice that could be heard by almost everyone in town. Homer edged the mule and wagon up to the intersection of Alamo and East Houston and turned left onto Houston. He continued at a leisurely pace for the two remaining blocks between his store and the courthouse square. All this time, L.V. was drawing attention– and a crowd–by loudly announcing that a famous Roman gladiator and his chariot were in Marshall and that he would demonstrate his prowess as a charioteer with a race around the courthouse square.

When Homer and his "chariot" reached the stop sign at the square, he told L.V. to brace himself for one helluva ride. A sizeable crowd had gathered at the square and the normally bustling area was quieted and stilled by their curiosity and sense of pending event.

L.V. hollered, "And they're off!" With that pronouncement, Homer-still standing–whipped the old mule with the reins and sent him flying. The mule reached full gallop in short order and the crowd responded with cheers and laughter. L.V.'s running commentary echoed through Marshall's downtown. As the wagon reached its first turn on the Northwest side of the square, the slop-filled barrels shifted and slammed against the wagon's railing sending fresh, stinky slop out onto the brick street. Homer kept pouring it on the mule and, since the square was really a circle, slop just kept flying out of the wagon, much to the delight of the enthralled crowd and the pet parade that followed the wagon.

As Homer brought the "chariot" to a halt at the end of his ride, he and L.V. waved victoriously to the cheering crowd and turned eastward onto Houston Street for the two-blocks-long, but triumphant, walk back to their store. Many of the crowd followed them back to the store where they talked and laughed with the two charioteers, petted the mule-turned-steed, bought snacks and sodas, and hung around chatting about the entertainment they had just witnessed.

Landy's mule fidgeted, pranced in place, and brayed loudly for some time after he was tied up at the store. One had to wonder whether the race around the square had nearly killed the mule or had given him a sense of power and/or excitement. For whatever reason, Landy seemed to be enjoying his fifteen minutes of fame. Landy stepped up beside his now-famous mule and posed for photographs, one of which appeared the next day in the News Messenger.

While most who witnessed the chariot exhibition seemed to have had a blast, not everyone was amused. The Marshall Police Department ticketed Homer $18 for driving recklessly and, later, charged him $25 for their having to clean up the mess he had strewn around the square.

Eubanks Quality Foods was doing nicely through the winter and summer of 1941, but Germany had cast a dark cloud over Europe and the cloud was spreading rapidly across America. Discussions about the likelihood and advisability of the United States joining our allies Great Britain and France in the war against Germany and its allies, Italy and Japan, were on every American's lips. Many believed we owed it to our allies to declare war on Germany while a great number demanded we stay out of it and let Europe solve its own problems.

That debate of war versus no war came to a screeching halt on December 7, 1941, when Japan unleashed a brutal surprise attack on America's naval fleet at anchor in Hawaii. The air attack killed 2,403 American servicemen, while only 55 Japanese airmen were killed by the stunned and militarily disabled Americans. The decision had been made for the United States. She had to defend herself and visit vengeance on its attackers. War on Japan was declared within hours of learning of Pearl Harbor. Germany, which had vowed to defend its allies should they enter wars with other countries, supported Japan by declaring war on the United States December 11, 1941.

Marshall, like towns and cities all over America, experienced a loss of many of its young, healthy men to military service. Thousands of young men rushed to volunteer for the war effort, and the draft, which had been authorized by Congress in 1940, swung into full operation after Pearl Harbor. Patriotism in America was at a fever pitch, but, at the same time, those hoping to stay out of the war did all within their power to avoid the draft and military service. "Draft dodgers," as they were labeled, were scorned by their communities, but they still preferred this derogatory name to risking their lives in war. Many men who had legitimate health issues that would earn them service exemptions lied about their health in order to serve. They were spurred on by a sense of patriotism, as well as a fear of being called draft dodgers.

Homer, who was thirty-four, a father of two, and a business owner, had no fear of being drafted, but he was one of those who worried about the stigma that was attached to those who didn't serve. His common sense told him he would be better off staying at home running his business and taking care of his family. However, there were other internal voices challenging that notion. He faced a dilemma.

## Homer's Wartime Dilemma

Despite the fact that the war raged on and dominated all aspects of life and business in America, Homer continued to operate Eubanks Quality Foods. Due to the monstrous demand for food and other products for our soldiers and those of our allies, it became increasingly difficult for the small grocery store to find many of the products it needed for its inventory.

The production of non-food items such as rubber, gasoline, footwear, clothing, typewriters, and even bicycles was almost totally dedicated to our war effort. The scarcity of goods available to civilians grew commensurate with America's involvement in the War. By the spring of 1942, the rationing of coffee, meat, cheese, butter, sugar, dried fruits, canned foods, lards, and oils was in full force. It became harder and harder to eke out a living from the store, just as it did for most commercial enterprises that dealt in goods and services not associated with defense contracting. Clearly, the battlefronts in Europe and in the Pacific were where the greatest dangers existed, but the homeland and its families were not exempt from sacrifice. Because so many men left their jobs and joined the service, the nation's families were also somewhat cash strapped. Homer and Zee decided to extend credit to the families of those who had joined the War effort. It was a noble gesture, but one that, at War's end, led to Homer's surprise and financial dismay. A significant number of those to whom he had extended credit never made an effort to repay their debt.

Homer agonized constantly over his indecision about enlisting in the service. His family needed him, but so did his country. His nephew, L.V., who was quite a bit younger than he was, joined the Marine Corps. Homer was proud of his nephew, but L.V.'s enlistment added to Homer's guilt about staying behind.

Finally, Homer's frustration boiled over. He and Zelma were

at the store one morning and Homer calmly took off his apron, folded it neatly, handed it to Zelma, and told her he was joining the Navy. His decision came as no surprise to Zee, as she had closely observed his growing agitation over staying behind while so many of his younger friends and family members had enlisted for the duration of the War. Homer and Zee had also had many discussions regarding the repercussions that would befall Zee and the boys if he enlisted. The main adjustment for the family, of course, would be dealing with the uncertainty about Homer's safety and the fact that Zee would not have his family leadership in raising the boys. Lastly, Zee would be faced with running Eubanks Quality Foods without Homer. The decision for the Eubanks Family was tough, just as it had been for all families sending their boys and men into the dark uncertainties of war.

In his last discussion with Zee before enlisting, Homer explained that he was sickened by those who checked into the hospital with phantom illnesses every time the draft bus rolled into Marshall. He was also angry at seeing how some of the rich and powerful pulled political strings to keep their sons from having to go to war. Homer explained to Zee that he did not want his boys growing up ashamed that their father had avoided military service when he was, in fact, capable of serving.

Homer joined the Navy in 1943. He was 35 years old. Though he had never been to sea, Homer joined the Navy as a sign of unity with that branch of the service after the devastation it had suffered at the hands of Japan at Pearl Harbor. Like most all Navy recruits, he was sent to San Diego for basic training and skills assessment. Because he was the oldest man in his training unit, he was quickly dubbed "the old man."

In his first letter to home, Homer told his family the "boy" in the bunk above him was a handsome young actor named Guy Madison. Homer confessed he had never heard of Madison but understood he was a real Hollywood heartthrob. It seems the actor had joined the Coast Guard, but, at that time, they were going through basic training with the Navy recruits. He added that

Madison's real name was Robert Mosely. He, also, commented that he was surprised at how many of the young recruits hadn't even started shaving.

Homer breezed through basic training and, in fact, was honored for having surpassed the other Navy recruits when tested for tolerance to high altitudes. He proudly carried a card in his wallet honoring him for his feat until his death. He also won accolades by being the first trainee to step forward and jump into the sea from the deck of an aircraft carrier, a distance of 57–75 feet, depending on the weight of the load the carrier is carrying.

Following basic training, Homer was sent to airplane engine maintenance and repair school, where he learned to become an aircraft mechanic. He served out the War in that capacity in San Diego and, for a short time, on Black Island, a tiny Pacific Island that served as a refueling spot for Navy pilots.

While Homer–like countless other soldiers, airmen, and seamen–missed his family terribly, he loved the Navy and the camaraderie and sense of common purpose that pervaded his time of service. The fact that he was stationed primarily within the United States greatly eased the hardship of his service. He was

**Homer (lower right) with friend Brown Lee McMahon and (top row, left to right) Homer Jr., Zelma, and Robert in San Diego, 1945**

basically out of the line of fire, plus he was able to visit freely with his family by telephone. He never regretted his decision to join the War effort.

Homer formed several friendships while in the Navy that lasted the rest of his life. He and his chief, A. J. Carr, became fast friends. While it was a bit unusual for officers and lowly seamen to become fast buddies, the fact that Homer and Chief Carr were about the same age took some of the edge off of their relationship. When Zee, Homer, Jr., and Robert visited Homer in San Diego in the summer of 1945, the Carrs spent considerable time entertaining the boys so Homer and Zee could spend time together. There are hints as to how they spent some of their time together, because Zee returned to Marshall pregnant with one who would become their third son, Paul Scott (Scotty) Eubanks, born April 18, 1946.

Homer also became close friends with a Chinese American in his outfit by the name of Dickie Doo-Dare. Like Homer, Dickie was an airplane mechanic. He and his parents had immigrated to the United State when Dickie was young and, even though he was educated in American schools, he still spoke with a pronounced Chinese accent. Homer was enthralled by Dickie's deep-rooted patriotism and the happiness with which he served and lived his life. Both Dickie and Chief Carr stayed in San Diego after the War. They also stayed in touch with Homer after he returned to Marshall in October of 1945.

Following his discharge at the Naval Air Station in Norman, Oklahoma, Homer returned to Marshall to resume running Eubanks Quality Foods. Homer, Jr. and Robert marched around Marshall in their dad's sailor hats and Navy neckerchiefs for months after his return. When Homer saw the pride his boys had in his War service, he knew he had done the right thing by enlisting.

A lot of things had changed in the short time Homer had been gone. Some were good. Some were not so good. On the downside, product and food cutbacks and rationing during the War had hurt a lot of businesses, including Eubanks Quality Foods. Profits were tiny if there were any profits at all. Large food chain stores like

A & P and Piggly Wiggly Super Market had moved into Marshall with lower prices and product choices small grocers like Homer couldn't match. Safeway was soon to follow.

Young veterans were returning to hometowns everywhere–including Marshall–in hopes of getting their old jobs back or searching for new ones if their old ones weren't available. Of necessity, many wives had become working wives during the war and numbers of those were reluctant to give up the jobs, with the accompanying money and independence they offered. Employers had figured out that women were great workers and, further, that they worked for lower wages than men did. These job frictions entailing pay scale differences between men and women, disagreements as to whether returning veterans were entitled to their pre-war jobs when they returned home, and the debate about whether wives leaving their homes and children for jobs was good for America caused some families marital problems and generally complicated the scramble that was on for post-war jobs.

More than a few vets had trouble slipping back into the flow of American life, particularly those whose service had cost them their jobs. Some returning vets fared better than others. Too many came home with brains that had been rattled by their experiences and the violence and hardships through which they had suffered and witnessed. The road back for those scarred and impaired veterans was both sad and very long.

Homer with youngest son, Scotty, after his first taste of a Hershey Bar, 1946

Of course, the greatest disruption to normality in American life was caused by the loss of loved ones to the Axis powers. Four hundred and twenty thousand Americans perished fighting in World War II, and approximately 675,000 of our servicemen were wounded. Very few families escaped the ravages of war. The Eubanks Family lost one of Homer's nephews, Dale, when the plane he was piloting went down while flying the infamous Burma Hump. Dale was the son of Homer's brother Aub.

All of the news wasn't bad following the war. America had been on the winning team, and Germany and Japan had been brought to their knees. The headiness that came with victory instilled a vibrant confidence in America and other allied nations. Military-related manufacturing switched back to the task of consumer production and had a large appetite for labor. Housing boomed, spurred on by the need for homes for our returning veterans. The government poured millions and millions of tax dollars into programs to help veterans assimilate back into America's mainstream. The nation viewed its returning veterans as heroes and treated them as such. The first home Homer and Zee ever owned was a small 900-square-foot wooden ranch-style house in Marshall's Southside. They paid $6,000 for the house in 1947 and financed it with a Veterans' Administration loan.

The United States had flexed incredible muscle in helping the Allies defeat the Axis Powers. It had proven it could quickly convert its domestic production to defense-related production and fill the skies, seas, and battlefields with massive amounts of effective armaments that could, and did, inflict mortal injury on armies that challenged its commitment to victory. While Hitler had ultimately been defeated with conventional weapons, America's development of atomic bombs and the dropping of them on the Japanese cities of Hiroshima and Nagasaki astounded the post-war world. Power of this magnitude, coupled with the manufacturing efficiency it demonstrated during the war, firmly established the United States as the most powerful nation in the world. Other nations, including potential enemies of the United

States, were momentarily awestruck and militarily paralyzed by the power of the bombs, although the USSR and China were quick to develop their own atomic weaponry.

Veterans came home after the War proud of the job they had done, and the nation's citizens shared in that pride because they rightfully felt as though they had been part of the war effort. There was a noticeable strut to their walk, and that strut carried over into the country's economy as it began firing on all cylinders rather quickly.

Homer was quick to notice that most returning veterans came home with well-deserved senses of self-worth derived from their service. Unmistakably, that sense created a strong bond between veterans. In countless cases, their shared national service overcame their heretofore dividing differences such as economic status, educational attainment, political leanings, and religious preferences. War service proved to be a great equalizer among the previously unequal.

Those who had seen action came home with varying degrees of mental baggage that, in some cases, were personality altering. Some sealed their memories within themselves and avoided talking about their experiences. Often these ex-GIs internalized their pain and scars to the point of suffering life-threatening anxieties that kept them in deep, dark places. Others found that talking about their experiences with others who had had similar experiences was cathartic and helped in the healing process.

In Marshall, the American Legion grew rapidly and became a popular place for veterans to gather and share war stories beneath the ever-present auspices of patriotism. Homer was a dedicated Legion member and loved the sessions where war stories were told by the men who had lived them. There existed an unspoken hierarchy among the vets with those who had distinguished themselves in battle at the top of the pyramid. The Legion also gave the emotionally wounded veterans a place where they could drown their memories and insecurities in the alcohol of their choice and with their brothers in war who understood their pain.

There were many heroes from Marshall, but Homer was most impressed by a man named Eugene Britt. Britt, who had been a house painter and handyman before the War, had distinguished himself through his bravery in some of Europe's fiercest battles. Once in the early 1950s, Homer took his three sons to meet Britt, who lived in a small, inexpensive, two-room apartment on U.S. Highway 80. Britt was divorced and lived alone. Homer introduced the shy warrior to his sons as a "true hero." As Britt sat quietly in his tattered wing-back chair just staring at the floor, Homer shared his well-documented heroics with his three sons. At Homer's urging, Britt reluctantly raised the lid on his old wooden footlocker that served as his coffee table and showed the awe-struck boys the countless medals, citations, and accommodations that validated his right to be called a hero. They were strewn haphazardly within the footlocker, but Homer removed them one at a time and had Britt recite the reason he had received each particular medal to his three boys. Homer hugged Britt as they said their good-byes. His three boys were struck silent by the magnitude of what they had just seen and the man they had just met.

Homer with his three boys, Homer Jr., Robert, and Scotty (in order of age)

When the manager of the local American Legion, Hubert McBride, closed the bar and ran the vets off at closing time, Homer often invited the hangers-on to his house for breakfast and more talking. Zee and the boys welcomed these warriors and, while Zee was preparing breakfast, the boys were treated to the real-life war tales told by the first-hand witnesses. Since the consumption of alcohol was a big part of these sessions, it was not unusual for one or more of the besotted veterans to sleep off their buzz on the Eubanks' sofa or floor. This gathering of vets at the Eubanks home went on well into the 1950s. Suffice it to say, many lasting friendships formed within this brotherhood of ex-servicemen. Eugene Britt made many of these sessions at Homer's house and, quite often, he was the one who slept on the floor or needed to be driven home. Post-War had not been particularly kind to this hero. Britt, the man who had helped win many important battles, was losing the one he was fighting against alcoholism.

The role Hubert McBride played in watching over the vets during their American Legion sessions was critical to easing the warriors back into America's new version of normal. He watched over them like a mother hen and when one of them had drunk himself unfit to drive home, Hubert called family or friends of the tipsy vet and told them to come get their man. Zelma received more than her share of calls from Hubert and was always grateful for his diligence.

Sometimes Homer would take his youngest son, Scotty, with him to the Legion. While Homer was drinking and socializing with his friends, Hubert often entertained Scotty by teaching him how to play pool or just talking to him. The young boy still remembers a musical ditty McBride often sung to him that went something akin to the following:

> Raccoon up the 'simmon tree,
> Possum on the ground.
> Possum yell to raccoon,
> Shake them 'simmons down boy,
> Shake them 'simmons down.

The exact words to that childish song are not important. The fact that Hubert took the time to sing them to the little boy was the important point.

No doubt, America was on a high after victory in World War II, but with each passing year, life marched toward a return to normalcy. The war eventually passed into America's rearview mirror. It, along with its many heroes, grew smaller and smaller as the engine of a rebuilding America raced ahead.

## Adjusting to Post-War America

The clinched fist of war had spared no nation or family from the harm it inflicted as it pounded the world from 1939 through most of 1945. When the War started, the American people–and most of those in other parts of the world–were still trying to regain their balance from World War I, the world-crippling Spanish Flu pandemic that had taken Homer's mother when he was a small boy, and the Great Depression. Additionally, many in America still had the gritty taste of the Dust Bowl in their mouths. The first half of the 20$^{th}$ Century had been a rocky ride, largely devoid of stability. The cumulative effects left by the serial hardships made for a toughness within the generation of those who had weathered them. Also, those hardships almost certainly brought some families closer together, strengthened the overall work ethic, and steeled the nation's patriotism. Hard times generally unify the citizenry in their efforts to survive and regain stability. Homer was one of the toughest, but he, too, felt the weight of the times on his shoulders.

While Homer had personally been spared the brutality of the battlefield, much of his life had been reshaped by the War. Zee, with the help of her and Homer's families, had kept their affairs in one piece while he was away. However, Zee couldn't stop the steady decline in their grocery business. New entries in the Marshall grocery business were huge, powerful chains that ran full-page advertisements almost daily. Their message to consumers was a good one that played well to the public. Simply put, they offered a greater variety of foods at better prices. The opening of Piggly Wiggly, A & P, and Safeway condemned many of the small, independent grocers to their ultimate failure the day they opened their doors.

Homer's return to Eubanks Quality Foods helped sales, but the handwriting was on the wall. His last big effort to rebuild his business culminated in a full-page ad he ran in the Sunday edition of

Marshall News Messenger June 6, 1948. In it, he credited Eubanks Quality Foods with having expanded its service facilities by adding a refrigerated fruit and vegetable case, a new ice cream case, and the most modern refrigerated reach-in case available that protected dairy products and eggs. He also announced the store had added a complete stock of frozen fruits, vegetables, poultry, and fish. The advertisement included photographs of himself, his Market Manager, Allen Power, the building, their new frozen food case, and a picture of the store's new Cushman motor scooter delivery vehicle. The caption under the photo of the scooter served as an announcement of the initiation of their new free delivery service.

Advertisement for Eubanks Quality Foods that ran in the Marshall News Messenger in 1948

The advertisement created a pronounced upward spike. However, the rise in sales eventually reached its apex, which happened to be at a level that was unsatisfactory to Homer. The store was profitable but did not produce profit enough to justify his staying cooped up behind a counter seven days a week, nor did the income he derived from it amount to enough to provide for Zee, their three boys, and himself. Those who knew him best also realized that Homer sought freedom from the strict regimen running his store required.

In late 1949, Homer sold his store to Judge and Mrs. J. G. Stauts. Stauts was a Justice of the Peace in the Grange Hall area of Harrison County, where he and his wife had run a small rural store with one gas pump for many years. The Stautses ran their new store for several years, but eventually closed it down to help their son in the new grocery store he had opened in another part of Marshall. The building that Homer had designed on the back of a paper sack eventually became an auto parts store.

Homer's first job after selling his store was as the assistant manager of Marshall's still-new A&P Supermarket. Zelma became the cosmetologist at one of Marshall's leading department stores. Their combined salaries exceeded the profits they realized from Eubanks Quality Foods after war broke out.

One day, while working at A&P, Homer saw a monstrously obese lady stick a full-sized ham up her dress and wedge it between her massive thighs. In a state of disbelief about what he had just witnessed, Homer watched the thief waddle past the check-out counters and out the front door without paying for the ham. He stopped her on the sidewalk and demanded she pay for the ham she had pinched. After her denial of theft, Homer demanded she spread her legs, thinking the ham would fall out. It didn't. He tried several maneuvers in hopes the ham would dislodge from her ham-clutching thighs, but they ended in futility.

Finally, tiring of his persistent efforts to free the ham from her thighs, she begrudgingly admitted she did, in fact, have a ham tucked under her dress. She then told Homer that if he really wanted the ham, he would have to stick his hands under her dress and retrieve it. A small crowd that had gathered on the sidewalk to watch the confrontation laughed at the apparent stalemate. She wasn't going to give up the ham easily, and he wasn't about to put his hands up her dress. Finally, a female checker named Florence walked up to the ham fancier from inside the store, waved a meat cleaver in front of her and told the thief to give up the ham or she would surgically remove it. That threat worked. Motivated by fear, she widened her stance even more, shook and twisted a little, and the ham fell to the concrete. Homer speared the ham with the cleaver and took it to the store manager's office and gave it to him. After hearing where the ham had been, the manager rinsed it off, marked it 30% off, and put it back in the meat case. They did not press charges against the thief.

Homer's tenure at A&P didn't last very long. One night when he was driving home from the American Legion, he was stopped and ticketed for drunk driving. His driver's license was suspended for six months. Since he lived several miles from A&P, he had to resign his position with them. Homer's brother Ab, who lived in Lubbock, told Homer his friend ran the Piggly Wiggly store in Lubbock and was looking for an assistant manager. Homer rode the train to Lubbock, interviewed for the job, and was hired. He moved in with Ab and Ora, Ab's second wife, who lived only two blocks from Piggly Wiggly, and spent his six months of having no driver's license in Lubbock. His younger brother, Cecil, also lived in Lubbock, where he owned the Grapette bottling company. Grapettes were grape sodas that were popular during the 50s and 60s. As penitence for his DWI ticket, the shamed Homer restricted his drinking to Grapettes. Zee and the boys visited him for a week at the three-month mark.

When his driver's license was re-instated, Homer returned to Marshall and went into the insurance business working for his long-time friend, Willard Coker. The new job gave Homer the freedom to move about he had so missed while running his grocery store, plus it paid him enough to make ends meet.

Homer was a terrific storyteller and was masterful with his use of humor, irony, and logic. Most of his stories were told at his own expense and, oddly enough, were true. One such story evolved from an event that happened as he was selling insurance. He had arranged an appointment with a couple to talk about life insurance. He arrived at their house right on time and knocked on the door. A lady Homer described as incredibly beautiful and sexy answered the door and invited him inside. Homer was stunned by how scantily dressed she was and it barely registered on him when she told him her husband had been unexpectedly called away and would be back in about an hour. She invited Homer to stay until his return, but he refused and said he would be back in an hour to meet with both of them.

Homer decided he would kill the hour at a local coffee shop. Images of the beautiful woman flitted in and out of his mind as he nursed his coffee. His fantasies blinked away when he noticed it was time for him to return to the couple's house. When he turned onto their street, he was relieved to see a car in the driveway, hoping it signaled the husband's return home. He mustered his most professional appearance and facial expression as he arrived at the front door and knocked. The still beautiful and still seductively clad woman answered the door. Her appearance again somewhat overwhelmed him and unexpectedly threw Homer off his game. His blood flushed to his cheeks as he struggled to find words to say to her. Finally, he sheepishly asked, "Has he got it in yet?" He had obviously meant to ask, has he got in yet? The beautiful lady answered the red-faced Homer by saying, "No, but he has returned home." Homer said this nightmare he had lived through had a happy ending. He sold them a very large policy.

Homer had a unique way of living his life. He was steady, but unpredictable. He was thoughtful, but impulsive. He was an understanding father to his sons but was a no-nonsense disciplinarian. He lacked a formal education but was extremely well-read and exceedingly wise. He was tough as an old saddle, but a sucker for a sad story. He was a paradox.

Homer and Zelma settled into their home on Marshall's South Grove Street and put the War behind them. They also settled into a comfortable lifestyle and enjoyed as much as life with Homer would allow.

## A Man of Axtion

When some men drink too much, they drink themselves handsome and make fools of themselves to nearby women. Others drink themselves tough and try to pick fights they usually can't win. When Homer drank a bit too much, he began to think of himself as wealthy and he sometimes bought stuff he really couldn't afford.

His purchases while in his alcohol-induced "wealthy" states weren't frequent, but they did lead to a new living room furniture set, a new 1956 Pontiac, and a twenty-one-inch Zenith television in 1951 that happened to be to first television set in our part of South Marshall.

Late one afternoon, when Homer returned home from running errands and stopping by the American Legion to wet his whistle, he parked his car on the street that ran beside his house instead of its usual place in the driveway. His sons met him at the front door and asked him why he had parked on Medill Street. Homer blew right past the boys and went straight into the living room. He answered them over his shoulder by saying, "You'll see. Now come on, we have work to do."

He told the boys to take all of the living room furniture out to the front yard and do it in a hurry. There was a sense of urgency to his voice so they got right on their assignment, figuring they would eventually find out what was going on. They noticed he had been drinking, but not enough to get loopy. Instead, he appeared to be fueled by the excitement of his mission.

The chairs, end tables, lamps and coffee table were no problem. The big green sofa was another story. In order to get it through the front door, two sharp turns had to be negotiated in a space that was not conducive to making sharp turns. After several attempts, Homer ran out of time and patience. He told the boys to have a seat while he retrieved some things from the garage. Three minutes later, he returned to the house and handed Homer, Jr. an axe, Robert a maul, and Scotty a hatchet. He then told his now-armed sons to chop that oversized son-of-a-bitch into pieces small enough to fit through the front door with ease. The boys attacked the sofa with a vengeance and, in short order, the sofa was piled in the front yard with the rest of the living room furniture.

Within five minutes of the sofa's removal, a delivery truck from McWilliams Furniture pulled into our driveway and delivered a new sofa, two over-stuffed side chairs, two end tables, a coffee table, and two lamps. Homer excitedly had the delivery guys arrange the new furniture just right and sent them on their way. Within minutes of their departure, Zee pulled into the driveway, killed her motor, and just stared at her living room furniture piled bonfire-style in her front yard. She walked into the house, took in her new living room furniture, hugged her three sons, and took her husband to their bedroom for a closed-door session. After some verbal venting by Zee, the two of them walked out of the bedroom arm in arm. It seems Homer had bought the new furniture as a surprise anniversary present for his Zee. She was clearly touched by his thoughtfulness and life returned to normal…for a while anyway.

Historically, after Homer and Zee married and had a family, he was a Chevrolet or Ford man. On top of that, he bought only used cars, shying away from paying the big prices of new cars. With these car-buying tendencies in mind, Homer's three sons instantly knew two things when their dad pulled in his gravel driveway behind the wheel of a brand new 1956 Pontiac. First, they knew he had been at the American Legion where he drank enough for the illusion of wealth to have taken over his senses and, secondly, they knew their mother would be as mad as a nest of wet hornets when she got in from work and discovered what Homer had done. They were right on both accounts.

When Zee got home, she exited her dark blue 1946 Plymouth coupe and slowly walked around the new sparkling green and white

Pontiac that now sat in their driveway. Knowing her husband as she did, she pretty well knew the score about the new car. She then came in the house, put her purse down, hugged each of her three boys, and calmly told her guilty husband she would like to speak to him in private. He gave his three sons an "oh hell" look and sheepishly followed Zee into their bedroom. She closed the bedroom door, listened to Homer admit to his latest financial folly, and then lit into Homer like a flock of buzzards on new roadkill. After about fifteen minutes of ranting, Homer and Zee emerged from the bedroom and she told their sons, "Come on. Let's see how this new Pontiac drives." Zee never stayed mad at Homer for long, and, somehow, they always managed to pay off his few extravagances.

The unexpected arrival of the new 21-inch television caused quite a stir at home. Zee had no sooner finished reading the riot act to her husband about spending money they didn't have on a television, when a crew showed up to install the forty-foot antenna that was required to pick up the television stations in nearby Shreveport, Louisiana. Zee was not exactly thrilled to learn of this added expense. Homer's explanation to Zee that if he had bought a sixty-foot antenna, they also would have been able to pick up stations from Dallas but he wanted to be frugal and "only" bought the forty-footer did not impress Zee. The entire television ordeal had temporarily strained relations between the husband and wife.

The new Zenith had also caused quite a stir in the neighborhood. Over a relatively short period of time, most all of our neighbors dropped by to inspect the television set and watch it for a while. People tended to inspect the "magic box" from all angles and just stare at it as though it was an alien from Jupiter. They were used to hearing people talk and sing to them from a wooden box called a radio, and the movies had paved the way for people to come to terms with the concept of seeing folks when they weren't really there, but seeing them less-than-life-size in a small box posed a real head scratcher to some.

Naturally, all of the kids in the neighborhood spent their afternoons hanging out on our living room floor watching westerns starring Bob Steele or Roy Rogers, Tarzan movies with Johnny Weissmuller, and space shows starring guys like Buster Crabbe or John Agar. On Saturday mornings, our floor filled up early, with kids fighting for front row seats for shows like Howdy Doody, Pinky Lee, and the Paul Winchell and Jerry Mahoney Show. When the shows came on, all bickering, chattering, laughing, and talking immediately ceased. All attention was hypnotically focused on the twenty-one-inch glass screen inside the huge wooden box.

Very early one Saturday morning, while the Eubanks family was still asleep, they were awakened by the sound of their new tv crackling and hissing from the living room. Homer went into the living room and was surprised to find a small boy sitting in from of the tv watching it intently. Back then, programming didn't begin until 7 a.m.. For the thirty minutes leading up to 7 a.m., each station ran a static image on the screen of what was known as a test pattern or test card. The test pattern, which was invented by RCA in 1939, consisted of geometric shapes which were used for the station to calibrate its monoscope before beginning program transmission. The young boy turned out to be Scotty's friend, Dickie Cole, who lived across the street from the Eubankses. Since there were no locks on the Eubanks' front door, Dickie had felt comfortable to enter the house, turn on the television, and watch the only thing on the screen–the test pattern.

Homer said hello to Dickie, who hesitantly broke from the spell of the test pattern long enough to return Homer's greeting, and then Homer went back to bed. Dickie was still seated in front of the Zenith when the family greeted the morning an hour or so later. Mother made them all breakfast, which they ate in front of the tv.

Television reception in the early 1950s was very iffy. The signal from Shreveport seemed to be strong for a while and then weak for a while. It was a minute-by-minute proposition. When it was weak, the image on the screen was littered with what was called "snow." Snow consisted of black and white electronic image-blurring spots that made watching a real challenge, if not impossible. During "snowstorms," viewers had to strain their eyes to watch the televised images hiding in the snow. Early television sets–or receivers–were far from perfect and frequently played havoc with quality viewing. Sometimes, the televised picture would roll top to bottom and, other times, the horizontal lines would capture the screen and ruin reception. There were control knobs for vertical adjustments that would sometimes stop the rolling for a while, and there was a knob called "horizontal hold" that usually straightened out the image. When either or both of these problems could not be stopped via adjustments, it was time to call the repairman who could replace the appropriate tubes in the set and restore a family's viewing pleasure.

The Weeks family was the next to buy a television in our neighborhood, so the band of tv-hooked kids in the area now had two spots to watch Howdy Doody and his horn-honking friend Clarabell the Clown. Terry Weeks was my best buddy and the two of us spent most of our waking hours together, whether playing, fighting, or watching television. One day, we were watching Terry's new Stromberg Carlson tv when it horizontal hold went haywire. Terry approached the tv and hit the side of the cabinet; a maneuver that had often proven remedial. This time, his repeated banging failed to bring Buffalo Bob back into visibility. In a fit of frustration, Terry kicked the front of the television. His kick didn't alter the sorry state of viewing, but it did cause a huge crack in the screen. Terry, fearing his dad's reaction, made a poorly thought out decision and turned the tv set around so it faced the wall, thinking he had successfully hidden the damage he had done from his parents. I quickly figured out that my buddy's strategy was a bad one and promptly excused myself and headed for home, knowing full well that Terry was in for some tough sledding when his dad got home from work.

Before long, television antennas punctured the sky all over Marshall's Southside and the rest of America. As a matter of fact, a story appeared in an East Texas newspaper in the early 1950s that reported there were eleven televisions in the small town of Tatum, Texas. The same article reported there were sixteen tv antennas up in the air in Tatum at the same time. Homer said the five folks with antennas but no tv sets were either optimists or people trying too hard to keep up with the Jones. For a while, having a television was a status symbol.

Television was here to stay and well on the way to eating what many folks believe to be an unhealthy amount of people's time and creativity. By being among the first to have a television, the Eubanks family had its fifteen minutes of fame, but when other families began to get their own televisions and the kids stopped relying on ours for their entertainment, I think Homer and Zee were glad to re-take possession of their living room.

Zee always maintained that Homer was a spend thrift when he drank too much. Homer countered that, if it had been up to Zee, they would have never bought anything. Both were right.

## Homer's Modus Operandi

On the outside, Homer usually appeared to be calm and almost passive. However, he was living proof of that old adage that proclaimed, "looks can be deceiving." There was a part of him that was pensive and contemplative for sure, but those tendencies spent a whole lot of time cowering in the back of his brain. For the most part, Homer's internal speedometer stayed on the far-right side of the dial. He was a pedal-to-the-metal man.

Homer's siblings used to joke that God had skipped him when He passed out patience, insisting that brother Paul had received his and Homer's share. Homer's action monitor was set on "let's go!" while Paul's rested on "if I must." Those action-oriented traits that his brothers and sisters had spotted in him when he was just a boy carried over into his adult life. When listening to one who had a story to tell or meeting one who needed help, Homer was attentive, interested, and very patient. It was when he encountered laziness, selfishness, or indecision that his hot buttons glowed red.

His three sons simply were not allowed to be lazy, selfish, or indecisive when their dad was around. All three of the boys violated these "Homer rules" from time to time, especially when he was out of town, but seldom skated free of Homer's justice. Robert, who was prone to long daytime naps as a teenager, took to finding hiding places– often outdoors-for his naps just to avoid scorching lectures from his dad on the evils of sloth. Through the years, his sons' inabilities to live up to some of his rigid standards gradually caused a noticeable softening in Homer's approach to how he disciplined his boys and how he judged others. He somewhat reluctantly accepted the fact that his sons were individuals in their own right and would never be fully compliant with his aspirations for his boys. He also recognized that his boys had talents and qualities he never possessed. Homer still worried, and once told Zelma that when he considered his sons' long-range futures, he was afraid Homer, Jr. would dream his away; Robert would sleep his away; and Scotty would play his away.

The Eubanks Family was extremely close. Every family member enjoyed the company of the other family members, but disagreements were fairly common. Disagreements among the boys were allowed, but when a settlement to the disagreement or argument was needed, the matter was taken to Homer, the grand arbiter. His rulings were final and could not be appealed. Zee was seldom called upon for arbitration. When she saw or heard an argument about to go physical, she never took sides. She simply stopped it with a loud, "shut up!" Her decisions weren't open for appeal either.

Homer's version of how to raise three, big, healthy boys differed somewhat from Zelma's. Homer wanted the boys to grow up tough, street smart, confident, and self-reliant. Zee, on the other hand, wanted her sons to grow up courteous, loving, and genteel. Honesty, strength of character, and the value of a good education were preached by both parents. One night when the entire family was seated around the supper table, Homer watched how Zee coddled their three sons. He slowly glanced around the table, and, then, exclaimed to his wife, "Zee, you're just plain old mommanizing these boys." Once he got that off his chest, everyone laughed and continued with their supper. To an extent, he was right.

Homer's interaction with his boys was normally judicial or action oriented. He would often push the living room furniture back against the wall, strap a boxing glove on one of each son's hands, along with one on his own. All four would stand in the middle of the room with their gloves touching. Next, Homer would holler "go," and everyone would start clobbering each other with their gloved hand. The rules prohibited hitting below the waist, biting, and kicking. After a while, Homer would stop the fight and make everyone take the glove off their right hand and tie it onto their left. Again, when he hollered "go," all hell broke loose, this time from the left hands. Zee either stayed in the kitchen, the bedroom, or the yard while these slugfests went on. She couldn't watch as the men in her life inflicted pain on each other. Homer viewed these sessions as fun and the toughening of his boys. In all of those free-for-alls, damage to furniture or the house only occurred twice. Once, Homer, Jr. knocked Robert through a section of sheetrock in the living room, wedging him between two of the studs in the wall. The other time, Homer knocked Homer, Jr. into an end table and broke a lamp. Homer took the heat for the damages from Zee, but, personally, considered the breakages just part of learning. In all fairness, the two Homers and Robert took it easy when hitting Scotty, who was much younger, smaller, and weaker than his dad and older brothers. They would hit him hard enough to rattle his brains and knock him down, but never hard enough to break bones or render him unconscious.

Another part of Homer's education plan for his boys was intellectual development, with an emphasis on common sense. He would often organize the living room chairs in a circle where he and his three sons faced each other. He would then name a subject or category and the four of them would take turns naming an example that fit the category. For instance, the category might be "Indian Tribes." The game would go on until all but one had exhausted the names of tribes they could remember. Robert was very creative when he was stumped. Rather than drop out of the game gracefully, he would make up a name and try to convince his dad and brothers of its existence. Homer never fell for his middle son's effort at cheating, but he did compliment his creativity.

Some of the other subjects that were used in the games included cigarette brands, breeds of cattle, Civil War generals, breeds of chickens, world capitals, species of trees, and two-letter words. The games were both educational and fun. Homer won most of them. What the boys learned from these games often proved useful within their circle of friends–often, but not always. Trying to impress his second-grade girlfriend one recess period, Scotty rattled off all of the names of breeds of pigs he had learned. It was a short-lived romance.

Homer took great pride in his yard. He was particularly proud of his many camellia bushes and 15–20 rose bushes. He patrolled them regularly to make certain aphids, caterpillars, and other leaf eaters weren't "bugging" his bushes. After finding a number of caterpillars on his prized rose bushes one Sunday afternoon, he recruited Scotty to check them daily and remove any of the worms chowing down on his rose leaves. He charged Scotty with this job because he had to go to Dallas for the week on business. To induce Scotty's diligence, Homer told his youngest son to put the caterpillars he found in a fruit jar and that he would pay him twenty-five cents for each one he had found when he returned from Dallas.

The financial incentive worked, and Scotty inspected the bushes daily. By Friday, he had put twenty-three caterpillars in the jar. When Homer got home Friday afternoon, he counted out the caterpillars and was a little taken back by owing his son $5.75 for just a pile of bugs. He instantly figured out that he had offered too high a bounty, even to his own son. Since he had to return to Dallas the following week, he re-negotiated the caterpillar contract with his entrepreneurial son. This time, he told Scotty he would give him ten cents for each caterpillar. In a poor bargaining position, Scotty accepted the deal. This week, he found 15 of the little critters, earning another $3.00.

When Homer thought about the fact that he had spent $8.75 in the last two weeks just to save a few rose bush leaves, he reacted in typical Homer style. He told Scotty that his job was to keep the caterpillars off the rose bushes, and that, for his good work, he would receive free room and board at the Eubanks household. Scotty maintained his caterpillar patrol, fully recognizing that he had received an order from his dad and that his only option was to comply. He lucked out because by Wednesday, the worms had quit eating and were busy encasing themselves in their cocoons on the road to becoming monarch butterflies.

Homer seemed to have an answer for every question and a solution for every problem. At least it seemed that way to his three sons. When he found out his two oldest boys had caught or developed tinea cruris, more commonly known as jock itch, Homer's solution to their problem was fast and sure, albeit quite painful. There were anti-fungal creams at that time which doctors recommended for jock itch. However, in Homer's judgement, they were expensive, slow acting, and equally slow to improve the symptoms that made the situation uncomfortable and unsightly.

Homer told the boys to fill the tub with hot–not warm-water, strip off, and wait until he returned from the neighborhood drug store. In very short order, Homer joined his naked boys in the bathroom and told them both to get in the tub. As they were inuring to the hot water, Homer pulled five bottles of rubbing alcohol from a paper bag. He quickly emptied each bottle into the bathtub and told the boys to stay in the tub until he told them they could get out. He then left them to soak-up his solution to their fungus.

In a very short time, both boys began to howl in pain as the alcohol penetrated their already-raw skin. Homer looked in on the crying teen-aged boys two or three times to make certain they were still submerged in the potion. They were, but they wanted out. After a few minutes, Homer told them they could get out of the tub, but that they couldn't dry off. The boys tore out running from room to room looking for relief from the intense burning. There was none. Finally, Homer, Jr. found an oscillating fan, plugged it in, and assumed a rather undignified position right in front of it. Robert soon joined him and the spectacle of two nude butts fighting for real estate in front of the old Emerson fan was worth the price of admission. After thirty or so minutes, God took mercy on the brothers and relieved their pain. Their previously infected areas were reminiscent of boiled lobsters, but the fungus that had caused them grief had been murdered by Homer's alcohol treatment. They were cured, and the boys dedicated themselves to never again letting tinea cruris fungus inside their underwear. Their Dad's cure was just too painful to suffer an encore.

Probably due to his upbringing where food was occasionally scarce, Homer did not tolerate picky eaters among his sons.

They had to eat what was put before them. That rule was easily followed because all three boys enjoyed all kinds of food. The relevant question in their minds seemed to be concerns over volume, not what was on the menu. The only time one of the boys drew the line in the sand about eating a particular food occurred when Scotty refused to eat the beets on his plate. Homer took his youngest son's rebellion as a personal afront and asked his beet-rejecting son to stay at the table after everyone else had been excused. Scotty sat with his arms folded across his chest and stared at his dad as the patriarch extolled the virtues of beets and why he had to eat them. After his impassioned logical explanation failed to convince Scotty to eat the beets, Homer changed his approach. He leaned across the table, stared deeply into the eyes of his defiant son, and calmly but firmly told his son, "You will either eat those beets or your skinny little ass will never leave this table." Scotty knew he had carried his protest to the end of the line. He ate the beets.

Food delicacies or expensive foods were extremely rare at the Eubanks house. Homer and Zee focused their culinary efforts on trying to fill up their boys rather than dazzle them with expensive foods. Quantity trumped quality. It was a strain on their budget just trying to satisfy the appetites of three large, athletic, growing boys.

The only time the family ate out was when they were on road trips. It was just too expensive to do so on a regular basis. However, one time, on the way to Alexandria, Louisiana, to visit Zee's parents and brother, the family pulled into a roadside café in the small town of Colfax. They took turns ordering their hamburgers until it came time for Robert to place his order.

To everyone's surprise, the middle son ordered shrimp, the most expensive item on the menu. Too embarrassed to cancel the shrimp order and replace it with a sandwich, Homer allowed it to stand. Robert seemed oblivious to everyone staring a hole through him because of his "selfish" order. He even had the temerity to throw out comments about how delicious the shrimp were as he scarfed them down. Homer was controlling his anger at Robert. It helped that

Zee was patting her husband on the arm to keep him from lighting into the oblivious Robert. Everything was stable at our table until Robert announced he was going to top-off his meal with a bowl of chocolate ice cream. That did it for Homer, who sprang from his chair, yanked Robert out of his, and dragged him outside. Scotty started to break for the door to watch Homer's sure-to-come tirade, but Zee made him sit back down. After an appropriate time, she paid the bill and they joined Homer and Robert in the car. Robert was curled up in a corner of the back seat and refused to talk. Homer was still seething, so conversation was in short supply for many miles. From that day forward, Robert and Scotty were forbidden to order for themselves. That rule would have been imposed on Homer, Jr. too, but he was already a student at LSU, having been awarded a football scholarship with the Tigers.

Homer's boys enjoyed watching their dad live his life. He was different from other dads, and he was fun and unpredictable. There was no doubt that Homer had a great sense of humor and was an enthralling storyteller. Friends of all three of his sons were drawn to Homer and loved his storytelling episodes. His ability to communicate with younger people in an understandable and humorous way led to his becoming the "go to" guy for many of the boys' friends when a disagreement arose between friends. Homer's rulings were respected by all concerned and were totally impartial, a fact that occasionally upset his sons.

Any accurate description of Homer's modus operandi was incomplete unless it included the words "impatient" and "decisive." One area where his impatience showed was when the family was on a trip. If the family was heading east, Homer always stopped in Waskom, Texas to fill his car with gas. Waskom, located sixteen miles east of Marshall, was the last Texas town before entering Louisiana where the gasoline tax was high and made gas expensive. Waskom gas prices were always the cheapest in the United States, because, in addition to Texas' lower prices, Waskom always had a gas price war going on. Waskom had a population of fewer than 1,200 folks, but it had 56 service stations. That fact made Waskom the subject of one of "Ripley's Believe It Or Not" cartoons in the 1950s. Homer's sister, Bon, had been the one to send that information to Ripley.

Eastward trips were rather frequent for the Eubankses because Zee's parents and her brother Blackie and his family lived in Alexandria, Louisiana. Additionally, son Robert moved to New Orleans when he graduated from college in 1960. It wasn't the trip or the gas stop in Waskom that caused Homer's impatience to flare. It was the fact that Zee always had to pee after traveling just 16 miles. The two-or three-minute wait for her emergence from the restroom after the car was filled and road-ready irritated Homer to no end. He took to calling Zee "Cadillac," implying that she was like a gas-guzzling Cadillac, in that she couldn't pass a gasoline station without stopping.

Homer smoked Camel cigarettes and was constantly dropping ashes on the dark green room-sized area rug in the family's living room. His efforts to use the ash trays that were scattered around the room left something to be desired. Zelma was constantly on his case about the ashes on the rug. He had no sellable defense to her constant scoldings, but he finally tired of them and figured out a solution. One morning while she was at work, he and the boys hauled the green rug out to the front yard, and he replaced it with a new grey rug. That afternoon, when she arrived home after work, Zee saw her nice green rug stretched out in the front yard as she wheeled into the driveway. When she entered the house and walked into the living room, Homer said to her, "Now, Zee, find those damn cigarette ashes."

Homer was a man who defied accurate labeling. The fact that he couldn't be slotted added to his aura.

## Homer Doses His Boys with Optimism

All parents teach and coach their children into adulthood whether they intend to or not. Good, loving parents teach principles, honesty, and many other traits that build character, enabling their children to add to the quality of mankind. Less conscientious parents unconsciously teach their children how to follow their footsteps into the realm of poor parenting. Parents without strong character cannot reliably teach solid character to their kids with any degree of expertise or expectation.

There are many cases of good parents turning out character-deficient kids and bad parents turning out character-rich kids. However, those are the exceptions to the rule, not the norms. Most all parents, in their sober moments, hope and wish for their kids to turn out to be good, wonderful, successful people, but wishing and hoping won't do the job. It takes some parental fire in the belly and "stick-to-itiveness" to pull off good parenting. In the final analysis, living a life that is rich in character that can be emulated by impressionable children gets the best results.

No parents are entitled to expect perfection from their offspring. It just won't happen. Besides, kids are aware of their parents' imperfections, so they know a parent is coloring outside the lines when the "do as I say, not as I do" parents expect perfection from their children. Do as I say, not as I do policies work until they don't.

Homer and Zelma were constantly trying to teach and mold their three sons into good men without destroying their freedom to achieve individuality. It was a tough line to walk for the parents. Whether on purpose or by accident, Homer and Zee had, more or less, divided teaching responsibilities about equally.

Zelma seemed to be responsible for teaching her rambunctious boys the values of loving and the evils of hating. She tried to teach them to respect others and to always be courteous. She taught table manners and the practice of giving people the benefit of the doubt. She preached sharing and the dangers of making hasty judgements. She despised selfishness and simply would not tolerate it. Zee worked at rounding off the sharp edges of her boys' tendencies, some of which Homer had accidently put there. Oh, she wanted her boys to grow up able to take care of themselves–physically, intellectually, socially, and mentally–but she bought into the notion that men could be tough as hell, while still being nice.

Homer's input into the molding of his sons' character was forthright and less subtle than Zelma's. His method of teaching his sons was basically through instruction rather than suggestion. He taught self-reliance, honesty, loyalty, and non-conformity when others were heading down the wrong path. He stressed the value of holding firm to one's convictions, even if the flow of the masses was in the other direction. Homer believed a handshake agreement was more binding than a legal one. At the risk of sounding corny and/or trite, Homer believed a man's word was his bond and should never be broken. The above-mentioned character traits were non-negotiable in Homer's eyes. They were instructions to his sons, not suggestions.

Maybe Homer's greatest gift to his sons was his spirit of optimism. Homer was indomitably optimistic. He lived his life thinking that if things could go right, they would. He loved Mondays, as he viewed them as opportunities to have a good week. The noted pessimist Murphy and Homer would have been mortal enemies had they ever met. Homer also echoed an old saying, "you will find what you are looking for." When Homer, Jr. faced leaving Marshall to take a job in another town, Homer told his son that if he went to this new town expecting to dislike it, he would. He added that he if moved there expecting to like it, he would. That message was part of Homer's dogma, and it filtered down to all three of his sons.

Non-Texans have long joked about how Texans brag about their state and think everything in Texas is bigger and clearly superior to anything available in other states. The admission of Alaska to the United States as our 49th state in 1959 dealt Texas pride a setback by replacing it as the largest state. Texas revered its status as the largest state in the Union, so when Alaska came in with its 586,400 square miles of land, it dwarfed Texas' 267,399 square miles and angered many Texans. Texans regained a modicum of their pride when word circulated that if all of the ice in Alaska melted, Texas would regain its number one status.

The pride Texans had (and still have) in their home state was and is real, usually to the chagrin of non-Texans. Texans were trained to love Texas from birth. Newborns often wore "Native Texan" tee shirts home from the hospital. Children studied Texas history and its heroes in elementary school, and every Texas child knew the words to "The Eyes of Texas," and knew the Bluebonnet was the state flower, the mockingbird was the state bird, and the pecan tree was the state tree, from an early age. Oddly enough, "The Eyes of Texas," which was written in 1902, is not the official state song of Texas. It is the alma mater of the University of Texas. It just resonated better with Texans than the official state song, "Texas, Our Texas" (1929) ever did. Ask most Texans what the title of the official state song of Texas is, and he or she will respond with, "The Eyes of Texas." Another demonstration of Texas pride striking at an early age occurred when Texas kids played king of the hill. In most of the world, kids charging up the hill hollered "charge." In Texas, they usually yelled "Remember the Alamo!"

Truth be known, Texans felt sorry for those born in "lesser" states. Homer wanted his boys to feel this pride in Texas and worked to instill it in all of them. On more than one occasion, he walked his boys into the backyard on a clear starlit night and told each of them to pick out a star. Once stars had been selected, he told the boys the star each had picked for himself was his lucky star. He went on to explain that his star would bring him great luck throughout his life. He then told each boy to thank that lucky star for his having been born in Texas. Homer cited the lyrics from the musical ditty about Pecos Bill, who was shooting out the stars, but "when he saw the stars declinin', he left one brightly shinin', as the emblem of the Lone Star Texas state." Whether it was hogwash, brainwashing, or the God's honest truth, the boys bought Homer's message and all three boys grew into optimistic men, all proud of being Texans.

A famous quote from Civil War Major General Philip Henry Sheridan, who was one of five generals who governed the territory that included Texas during reconstruction, earned the eternal ire of Texans when he said about Texas, "If I owned Texas and Hell, I would rent out Texas and live in Hell." A glance at the Texas-hating General Sheridan's biography reveals he was born in New York and died in Massachusetts. A Texan would tell you the General got half of his wish. It appears as though Homer and Zelma were proud of how their boys grew up. They knew all three were imperfect in many, many respects, but all things considered, they appeared to be proud of their boys. On the other side of the coin, the three boys were unquestionably proud of their parents.

## Homer the Teacher

Homer's three sons were in constant pursuit of understanding their dad. He was quite different from the dads of their friends, and his approach to life seemed to be the result of a Mulligan's stew of hard knocks, family love and loyalty, an internal fire that gave him resiliency and toughness, a bright and quick mind, and an innate ability to do the right thing in any circumstance that arose. Add an unyielding sense of optimism and you had the man his sons perceived him to be.

His growing-up years and the hardships he had to deal with while doing so were almost unfathomable to his sons: mesmerizing and fascinating, but almost unfathomable. That odd stew that was his elixir of life nourished a raw boy who grew into a man who was a formidable combination of knowledge, wisdom, and reliable instincts.

Homer never offered himself as perfect. Far from it. He was quick to point out his own weaknesses and tried to use them to convince his sons why they should not allow those same weaknesses to eat away at their quality of life. He recognized the problems his sporadic weakness for alcohol had caused on occasion in his own life and shared them with his sons in hopes it would encourage abstinence, or at least moderation, in his boys. He disliked his own cynicism and his tendency to prejudge others. His teachings against these personal weaknesses were strong, but the genetics he passed on to his boys sometimes proved immune to his teachings. Homer's belief that boys needed to earn their own manhood through their experiences led to a permissiveness that sometimes conflicted with his teachings. Homer, like most conscientious parents, tried to pass the best of himself on to his sons. Historically, that parental desire falls a bit short of its mark. Current events, the individuality of children, and, of course, genetics, often conspired to derail a parent's best teaching efforts.

With his eighth-grade education, Homer clearly did not fit into the academic definition of an intellectual, but he was keenly intelligent in that he had the ability to acquire and apply new knowledge and skills. He still had his blind spots and proved on more than one occasion that he was capable of doing dumb stuff. However, few could say he was not a knowledgeable man, as he repeatedly demonstrated that he possessed an in-depth mental understanding of the information he attained. It should also be noted that he was a quick study which enabled him to easily understand new information and changing situations.

While Homer's knowledge base and his constant hunger for new information always impressed his family, they were most impressed by his wisdom. Wisdom is often defined as the quality of having experience, knowledge, and good judgement. Homer got an A+ on that test. He was wise, and he amazed his idolizing sons with his seldom erring wisdom.

Homer was the kind of person who dropped little pearls of wisdom into discussions on a regular basis and when they were least expected. His boys often wished they had followed him around with a notebook and pen in hand just to record his bits of wisdom and his witticisms. One time, he was holding court with his boys and he told them he didn't expect perfection from them. He went on to say that no one since Christ had been perfect, but that didn't stop him from hoping that four groups of folks were perfect: preachers, doctors, judges, and plumbers. He knew his desire for perfection from these people was impractical, but that didn't stop him from hoping.

Most parents want their children to grow up to be happy adults. Homer was no exception. He believed an optimistic outlook gave people a leg up on achieving happiness so he worked hard to instill a sense in his boys that said, "if things can go right, they will." He admonished his sons never to waste their limited time on earth running through life looking for ways to escape from bad things, bad people, sadness, grief, and challenges that seemed unmeetable. Instead, he counseled that happiness in life comes from accepting the truth and moving on.

Each of his boys learned early on when he started driving that when his dad asked him where he was going, he should answer the question directly. He should never say, "I don't know," or "nowhere in particular." Robert once answered the "where are you going" question from his dad with a shoulder shrug and one of those imprecise answers. Homer shook his head and told him, "if you don't know where you're going, any road will get you there." After a mini lecture from his dad about how a man needs to always know where he is going and why he is going there, Robert revised his loosy-goosy answer and said, "I am going to pick-up Pinky Hughes, Dick Fisher, and Gilbert Shivers, and we are going to ride up and down Grand Avenue looking for girls with loose morals. If we find none, I will be home by eleven feeling very disappointed." Homer nodded to Robert and added, "Good luck. See you at eleven."

Since all three of Homer's sons were better-than-average athletes, it was common for the entire family to be outside passing the football, playing catch with the baseball, or involving themselves with various competitive contests. Homer and his brothers and sisters had grown up with no toys, sports balls, baseball mitts, bicycles, little red wagons or other diversions. Their focus had been on working in the fields and, besides, disposable income was a stranger that never visited their small farmhouse. While Homer never complained about growing up without having learned to play ball or other games, he took a good bit of ribbing from his boys about his inability to ride a bike or catch and throw a football or baseball.

One afternoon, Homer and his three boys crossed the street and went into the Weekses' backyard to play a game of basketball. The Weekses were away from home and everyone knew they wouldn't mind sharing their basketball goal with the Eubankses.

Homer had never played basketball and had no idea what the rules were. After a short, rushed explanation of some of the rules, Homer hollered, "Play ball!" He knew the object was for his team to score more goals than the other team did and that it was okay to try to keep the opposition from scoring. The problem was that Homer had no appreciation for the finer points of defense and he would simply grab the guy with the ball or throw a shoulder into him if he tried to shoot. The game was stopped numerous times by the boys, who tried to teach their dad some of the game's finer points. Their attempts to teach Homer a gentler version of basketball fell on deaf ears. They soon realized their dad had left any finesse he may have had in Peno Bottom, Oklahoma. Their game evolved into one that had no rules. Keeping score fell by the wayside and their attention turned to survival until the game was finally called due to fatigue. As they walked home, the boys realized their dad believed that if one was to compete at anything, he should play to win.

Homer wasn't much at playing ball and couldn't ride a bike or turn a cartwheel, but he showed off one of the skills he had learned as a teen one morning while the family was riding down to his sister Bon's house on Caddo Lake. When we turned off Farm-to-Market Road 2606 onto a one lane blacktop road, we had about a mile to go to get to her house. The railroad track that ran from Jefferson to Karnack crossed that little road and, once in a blue moon, a freight train would be coming through. Such was the case this particular morning so we had no choice but to wait its passage out.

After a couple of minutes, Homer broke his family's boredom by telling everyone to get out of the car and follow him. We all walked up near the train and Homer told us all to watch his technique. He then told Zelma to pick him up in Karnack. There was no ensuing discussion. Homer, in his mid-forties, started loping alongside the train and after about 100 or so yards, he grabbed onto the ladder of a passing boxcar. His legs swung out behind him and then swung forward enough for him to attach his feet to a rung of the ladder. He looked back at his stunned family and waved three fingers at us to let us know he was alright. When the train cleared our crossing, Zee turned the car around and we drove the seven miles into Karnack. The train and our car arrived in Lady Bird Taylor Johnson's little hometown of Karnack at about the same time and, as it slowed while passing through town, we saw our dad jump off the train and run along beside it until his loss of momentum brought him to a standstill.

We were in shock at having witnessed Dad's daring feat. As was said before, he was a different kind of dad and, it's fair to note, that not everything he taught his sons was necessarily practical.

## Homer's Rules

When Homer's and Zee's middle boy, Robert, graduated from college and was about to start his drive to New Orleans where he had accepted a job teaching high school biology at the Crescent City's Fortier High School, Homer's last advice to him was, "Remember what I've always told you, you will always find what you are looking for. If you expect to like New Orleans, you will. If you expect to enjoy your job, you will." It was a bit of advice he often urged his sons to follow. That admonishment to Robert was 100 percent pure grade Homer. It underscored his core belief that a bad attitude was a major deterrent to one's happiness. Robert did, in fact, love New Orleans, and he loved teaching. His dad was right. He found what he expected to find, and he never returned to Texas from South Louisiana.

All parents have rules for their children. Some have strict and confining rules, while others have very lax rules. However, for the most part, parental rules are designed to protect their children, teach their children responsibility, lighten the parents' worry load, and keep their kids out of jail. Homer was no exception. He, in collaboration with Zelma, had rules, too. Many of those rules, such as ones dealing with curfews, school grades, obeying your parents, lying, theft, murder, etc. were rules shared by many parents.

Homer's rules were often more far-reaching than those issued by most parents. They weren't just rules he expected his boys to follow, they were teachings, too; teachings and rules wrapped in a package of high moral and ethical standards. Each rule seemed to be a plank in building a foundation of character.

Many of Homer's rules focused on teaching Homer, Jr., Robert, and Scotty to be men of their word. It wasn't a complex issue in Homer's mind. To him, it was as simple as doing what you said you would do and doing so in a fair and straightforward manner. Homer lived the old adage, a man is as good as his word. This concept was drilled repeatedly into the heads of his sons. The concept had sub-sets which he also stressed. For example, he told his sons that if they borrowed money and couldn't pay it back when it was due, to go to their lender and own up to their shortcoming. He said to acknowledge their debt and to tell the lender when and how they could pay him back. Homer had another rule under the heading of "borrowing." He instructed his sons that if they ever borrowed a tool, a lawn mower, a car, or any other item, always return them on time, re-gassed, and sparkling clean. It was part of his philosophy that called for being honest, thoughtful, and truthful.

At the time Homer was coaching his sons about how to handle debt, the value of a handshake, and what to do when they couldn't pay his debts on time came about the time credit cards were becoming available. Homer had a couple of gasoline company credit cards and a Sears Revolving Credit account but, for the most part, credit was extended to patrons by merchants based on the character and reputation of the applicant. A firm handshake sealed the credit arrangement. The first credit card was issued in 1950 by Diners Club. It was pretty much reserved for the wealthy and used by those who traveled or entertained a great deal. It was a bit of a "look how rich I am" symbol for those who had one. American Express and BankAmericard came on the scene in 1958 and their popularity spurred the use of widespread credit soon thereafter. Prior to their rampant use, obtaining credit was an eye-to-eye, one-on-one arrangement, and honoring or not honoring that debt was a matter of character.

Homer was not impressed when he heard someone say, "I meant to do this or that but just didn't get around to it." To him, unfulfilled intentions were totally useless. He told his boys, "Intentions aren't worth a damn without action, and the woods are full of folks with good intentions, and that is where they should stay."

He was also dubious about the value of saying I'm sorry after a major mistake and expecting full exoneration. He noted that prisons were full of felons who were sorry for their felonies. Being sorry for killing someone, didn't make the victim less dead. He acknowledged that saying I'm sorry was better than saying nothing after erring or wronging someone, but he was quick to point out that it seldom absolved one from having screwed up. He never expected perfection from his sons, but he did expect effort and improvement.

Respect was a frequently discussed topic at the Eubanks household. Perhaps still in the afterglow of World War II, Homer expected everyone to show respect for our United States and its flag. It wasn't a hard sell for him as his sons, and most all of America, had immense pride in their nation, its flag, and the freedoms for which it had fought. Respect for the law was coached and expected, too.

Homer generally believed young people should respect their elders, but he fell short of making that a hard and fast rule. A firm believer that respect had to be earned rather than just granted, Homer knew many adults that were not worthy of respect and he gave his sons a loose rein in awarding respect to their elders. He did lean toward the respect for your elders side of the equation if it was a close call, but it wasn't set in concrete.

As has been previously pointed out, Homer's three boys were better than average athletes. Homer, Jr. was an excellent track athlete. He held the local high school high jump record for more than 40 years and he was fast on his feet. Homer went to watch his son compete at the big district track meet and was thrilled when he won the high jump blue ribbon. His son's next event was the 100-yard dash. Homer, Jr. was fast off the line and was leading at the halfway mark, but he glanced over his shoulder and saw one of his competitors streaking up behind him. The boy passed Homer, Jr. and it was clear he was going to win the sprint. In disgust and mad at himself, Homer, Jr. took his foot off the pedal and coasted across the finish line in fourth place. Homer just shook his head and waited behind the bleachers for his son to join him.

When the two Homers came together, the dad congratulated his son for his high jump ribbon, but the discussion wasn't over. Homer told his son that losing the 100-yard dash was of no concern. He went on to say victory is sweet but not nearly as important as giving your total best effort to a challenge whether you win or finish dead last. He put the subject to rest by adding that victory is in the effort, not crossing the finish line first.

On the drive home from the meet, Homer raised the subject of his son having looked over his shoulder during the race and allowing the sight of the runner gaining on him to impede his effort. He then quoted the old baseball great, Satchel Paige, as saying, "don't look back, something might be gaining on you."

One of Homer's often repeated rules/teachings involved the tendencies of average people to follow the crowd without knowing why they were doing so. He understood the need for conformity when the masses were heading in the right direction. He cited patriotism, belief in God, and obeying the law as examples of when conforming led to rewards or character building. But, in general, Homer was never very comfortable cozying up to the idea of conformity.

He cited lynchings, looting, and general mediocrity as examples of societal conformity. He endorsed thinking outside the box long before it became an over-used idiom in American society. He supported his call for non-conformity by pointing out that medical breakthroughs, inventions, and many design and systemic improvements were the result of non-conformist thinking. He was afraid to tell his boys outright to lead lives of non-conformity, but he wasn't afraid to tell them to be independent thinkers.

Most every Sunday night, Homer gathered all of the shoes his family wore that were made of leather into the living room. He then laid out on newspaper spread on the rug all of his shoe shining polishes, brushes, and shine rags. It was shine time and all the boys joined their dad in a shine-a-thon. It was an enjoyable time of talking, laughing, and buffing. Homer told his boys often to keep their shoes shined and their fingernails clean if they wanted to make a good impression.

When all of Homer's rules and teachings are laid out in one place, it appears as though living with Homer was so fraught with do's and don'ts that life for his sons must have been like bootcamp. That feeling or assumption is totally false. The truth of the matter was that his boys loved to talk with their dad and were never in a rush to leave a discussion with him. He taught his boys by teaching them, not preaching to them. He made his teachings real by using humor and real experiences. He gave prime examples of why his rules made sense. He would allow his boys to disagree with him, but not to disobey him. They did so on occasion but it wasn't because they disagreed with him. It was because they just flat out defied him. Truth be known, Homer had his boys under his magic spell. They loved him and enjoyed spending time with him and listening to him. He didn't try to be friends with his boys; he tried to be a good father to them.

## Pig's Feet, High Noon, and Alley Cat

As generations age, they cling to many of the customs, preferences, and habits that gave them pleasure or comfort in their younger years. They do so at the risk of being teased or laughed at by those of the succeeding generation. The kids just can't fathom why their parents retain these "antiquated" oddities that are now so passé. Without knowing it, the younger folks are in the process of developing their own list of preferences and habits to which they will retain loyalty even in the face of ridicule from their children. What tasted good to them as kids will taste good to them as adults. What they enjoy doing as kids will likely give them pleasure when they are adults.

Homer's early life had been virtually devoid of frills and extravagances. It had been a life filled with love, but a life devoted to working for the necessities with extraordinarily little time left over for dreaming of what was always out of reach. Like most kids, Homer had become inured to his and his family's lifestyle. Reality had a way of imposing itself on those stuck in its sometimes-uglier confines. Homer and his siblings never felt needy or spent time wishing they had more. In truth, they really had no idea of what they were missing. Instead, they relished being with each other and they found many ways to have fun and laugh together.

Most everything he experienced after he left home was something that had been unavailable to Homer in his youth. When he stepped away from his family's small house on their sharecropping farm in Peno Bottom, Oklahoma, he stepped into a world he had not experienced before and, for the most part, knew little about. Homer was pragmatic. He liked where he came from; he liked where he was; he liked where he was going. He didn't bring a lot of baggage from his old life with him into his new one.

He did, however, bring a few tastes and old habits from his past; not many, but a few.

When he was growing up, he viewed pickled pig's feet the same way a rich man might view caviar. It was a rare treat and a delicacy to his untrained palate. His love of pickled pig's feet (complete with hooves) remained a favorite of Homer's throughout his life. If was a love that his wife and boys were slow to embrace. While, in truth, they didn't taste nearly as bad as they looked and smelled, his boys teased him ruthlessly about his love for them and made him promise to never eat them in front of any girls they brought by the house.

There were very few snack foods or leftovers to be found in the Eubanks kitchen when Homer was a youngster. When he and his siblings needed a snack between meals, their options were few to none. The one thing they could usually find to quiet their rumbling bellies was a glass of buttermilk and biscuits or cornbread to break apart and put in it. Buttermilk with cornbread in it was Homer's go-to hunger killer from childhood on up. Zee and their boys developed a taste for this filler, but it, like the pickled pig's feet, was never to be enjoyed in front of company.

The Eubanks kids had grown up on the farm eating lots of pork, potatoes, fresh vegetables, biscuits, and a variety of other homemade breads. Of course, various kinds of gravy were usually on the menu, too. In the winter, the vegetables and fruits that were eaten were those that had been put up (preserved) when they were in season. Preserved foods were stored in the family's root cellar in Mason glass-topped fruit jars until they were used. The root cellar kept foods away from sunlight and at a constant temperature year-round.

Dessert was a rarity except for syrup and jam with a little sugar sprinkled over it. Special sweet treats included berry and fruit cobblers, but they were only available when the family experienced bumper crops in one of the fruits or berries. Watermelons were common around Peno Bottom so the Eubankses had their fill of them in summer months. At most any time during summer, one could find two or three melons submerged in the nearby creek to cool them before being eaten.

When Homer told his boys about the foods on which he had been raised, he spoke most highly of red-eye gravy, maple syrup, cobblers, and biscuits. That list of favorites didn't surprise the boys because they were still staples at their house. Homer professed that there was not a food he did not like. He raised three sons who could say the same thing far into their adult years. Not eating something that was put on your table or plate was not an option available to the Eubanks boys. In general, the Eubanks boys rarely had questions about what a particular food was or if they had to eat it. Their only question was whether there was more of it in the kitchen. Homer, himself, was not a big eater. His boys were big eaters, but Homer made certain the foods were equally distributed to his sons.

His three sons had a good understanding of the foods their dad enjoyed but never knew much about what their dad did or did not like in other parts of his life. He seemed to keep his list of wants small and the boys felt as though his list was dictated by how much disposable income he had. They knew he and Zee had major limitations on their money so, for the most part, the boys self-imposed limitations on their own wants and desires.

One thing Homer loved was ice cream. A highlight for any semblance of a family reunion was the making of ice cream. The only negative thing about making homemade ice cream was that it took so long to freeze. Obviously, family reunions weren't weekly events so Homer fed his passion for ice cream by buying mellorine, a fake ice cream that cost anywhere from 15 to 25 cents per half gallon less than real ice cream. That savings made the Eubanks Family a mellorine family. Mellorine became quite popular in the early 1950s because of its cheapness, but no one ever thought it could hold a candle to the real thing.

When television entered the Eubanks household in 1951, Homer greeted it with mixed emotions. He enjoyed watching it, but he felt a bit guilty when he sat before it because just sitting had never been an option for a man who always stayed busy. Although he let it pass most times, it clearly bugged Homer when he came home and found his three sons lolling in front of the big Zenith. He just could not imagine that there was nothing beneficial they could be accomplishing with their time.

Gradually, television became okay to Homer. His favorite shows were the Wednesday and Friday Night Fights, professional football on Sundays, *Dragnet*, *You Are There with Walter Cronkite*, and *Gunsmoke*. He watched other programs, too, but he could not stand the comics Milton Berle, Red Buttons, or Red Skelton. Liberace wasn't a favorite either. He thought the comedians were just silly, and he could not stand the fact that they laughed at their own jokes. However, he liked Jackie Gleason. Homer was plain uncomfortable with Liberace's effeminate ways. He ceded television control to Zelma when Lawrence Welk, *The Ed Sullivan Show*, *Queen for A Day*, *This Is Your Life*, *The Hit Parade*, and Liberace came on. Homer preferred John Cameron Swayze and Edward R. Murrow to Huntley and Brinkley because he thought Chet Huntley and David Brinkley were too liberal.

To his boys' knowledge, their dad went to very few movies, only two of which earned five stars from him. In 1952, he and Zee went to Marshall's Paramount Theater and saw *High Noon*, starring Gary Cooper and Grace Kelly. Perhaps because the movie featured a man (Cooper) standing up to evil even when his own friends refused to help him, *High Noon* became the standard by which he judged all other movies. The movie told of a man in the mold of how Homer saw himself.

The other movie Homer saw and liked was *Bad Day at Black Rock*, starring Spencer Tracy and featuring an all-star cast of Robert Ryan, Lee Marvin. Ernest Borgnine, Walter Brennan, Anne Francis, and Dean Jagger. In the 1955 movie, Tracy played the role of a one-armed war veteran returning to his home of Black Rock after the war. It featured the themes of individual integrity, group conformity and complacency, and civic responsibility. It was more than a tale of good versus evil. It reached deeply into the character of a town and its people and the weaknesses that take control when civic lethargy is allowed to dictate the terms of life. As did *High Noon,* this movie hit the hot buttons of Homer's feelings about fairness, accepting responsibility, and standing firm on your principles.

Because of the age span of his three sons–thirteen years between Homer, Jr. and Scotty–Homer got an earful of all the popular songs of the 1940s, 1950s and early 1960s. While he really wasn't into music and couldn't dance a lick, a few of the songs he heard became his favorites. It's easier to list his favorites than to discuss them.

A list of favorites included "Mule Train," Frankie Laine, 1949; "Wheel of Fortune," Kay Starr, 1952; "High Noon," Frankie Laine, 1952; "Mexican Joe," Jim Reeves, 1953; "Tweedily Dee," Teresa Brewer, 1955; "Green Door," Frankie Vaughan, 1956; "Moonlight Gambler," Frankie Laine, 1956; "Rinky Dink," Dave Baby Cortez, 1958; "Alley Cat," Bent Fabric, 1962; *Sil Austin Plays Pretty for the People* (album) Sil Austin, 1959

It should be noted that Homer's favorite song on the Sil Austin album was "Danny Boy." Austin was a jazz saxophonist who had attended the Juilliard School of Music.

Homer's taste in literature stayed pretty close to books that dealt with history. When at home, he read books about America at war and, when on the road, he read novels about the Old West. Perhaps oddly, he loved the writings of Marcus Aurelius, too, and cherished the book of his writings given to him by Homer, Jr. as a birthday gift.

The week before his death, Homer moved into a twin bed in his son Scotty's bedroom because Zelma had the flu. At that time, Scotty was reading a group of novels by James A. Michener for a school project. He had read *The Bridges at Toko-Ri* and was now reading *The Bridge at Andou.* Homer started reading the Korean War novel, *The Bridges at Toko-Ri* (1954), while Scotty continued reading his non-fiction book about the Hungarian Revolution that was put down by the Russians after a bloody five-day battle in 1956. When the father and son finished reading each night, they would take turns telling each other about what they had read. That time together proved most enjoyable and enlightening to both. Their bond was strengthened by learning of each other's intelligence and observations. A few days after literary night sessions, Homer told Zee that the discussions had proven to him that his youngest son would do well in life.

Homer was fun. He had fun, too, but his fun seldom revolved around partaking in organized entertainment opportunities. He had not learned to lean on other people for his fun. Growing up, his fun was shared with his siblings, not trips to town, dances, movies, sports, etc. As an adult, his fun sprung from good times with his family members and "bull" sessions with the folks with whom he enjoyed spending time. He had the kind of personality that provided the fun for others, and he just wasn't reliant on others for his fun.

## The Paradox He Was

As Homer eased into his 50s, his mellowing became noticeable. He still had moments of high energy, exuberace, and rowdiness, but his family could see the changes his aging was bringing about. There was no alarm within his family because by the norms of the day, he was at the age when slowing down was supposed to begin occurring. It is commonly pointed out these days that today's 70-year-old is yesterday's 50-year-old. Homer would have made a terrific poster boy for that observation.

As has been frequently pointed out, Homer was keen to teach his boys as much about life as he could. He enjoyed his role as teacher and his sons enjoyed being his students. One of the difficult-to-understand lessons he tried to impart to his boys was that there were countless choices each must make throughout his life, and the collection of those choices and their results would define how each one's life and the quality of living he enjoyed turned out. He said that impulsive decisions made in the absence of serious thought could lead to choices that were harmful, wasteful, and ones that often served only to steer one off the road leading to happiness. He further told his three boys to see every choice they had to make as an opportunity to enhance their lives, and never to dread a decision because they feared making the wrong choice. His theory was that indecision was as harmful as making a poor choice.

Homer also reminded his sons that the world was a place of extremes, and life was akin to a balancing act in which the participants tried to avoid them. His examples included: up and down, long and short, left and right, for and against, right and wrong, love and hate, and many more vast range of options that colored a lifetime. The delicate part of this lesson he tried to impart was teaching his boys that, while they should generally avoid the outer edges of the extremes, they should also avoid living a life confined to the middle of the road. He placed very little value on living a life in which achieving mediocrity was the goal. The freedom to move out of the safe and neutral zone was a freedom to be cherished. He maintained that circumstances would often arise in a life that caused one to express one's beliefs and take a stand. Courage and character should be given a loose rein to lead one in those decisions. These were hard lessons to understand and to learn, but Homer thought they were worth the effort. He taught from experience, having lived parts of his life closer to the extremes than was advisable.

While Homer watched his sons grow into manhood, his sons watched him grow as a father. They had witnessed the smoothing out of the jagged edges that so defined their father when he was younger. Their dad had slowly allowed his wisdom to conquer his impulsiveness. He had learned to allow his sense of humor to soften situations against which he would have struck out at previously, and he learned to temper the harsh judgments he would have rendered when he was younger. His cynicism was more subdued. The Eubanks family's dad had learned to sit back in his chair and listen rather than sit on the edge of his chair and talk. His hair had begun to thin and he grayed around his temples. The gray helped to tame his rugged and somewhat wild looks. He did, however, still wear the scars and subtle signs of hardship that had so colored his younger years. They were just toned down by the kinder and gentler looks worn by the mature Homer.

With age, Homer had clearly calmed most of his wilder impulses, yet he still showed signs of the old Homer on occasion. These reversions to his old habits were wholly consistent with the paradoxical nature of his life. The man who showed up at a number of his youngest son's baseball games drunk as a skunk was the same man who went several years without drinking alcohol and served as a deacon at the First Baptist Church, sung in the Baptist Brotherhood's choir, and filled pews on Sundays with his friends and family.

That same man who had made his living and a reputation for toughness by beating up bad guys when he was younger had morphed into a peace-loving homebody, but still carried a sawed-off pool cue under his front seat in case he ran into trouble.

Just the week before he died, he and Homer, Jr. were working in the Tyler Area and stopped one evening at a roadside bar and grill for supper. As they were eating, a scuffle broke out in the end of the place where the bar and dance floor were located. Homer, Jr. noticed his dad was getting fidgety and kept glancing toward the trouble area. As the scuffle picked up steam and the ruckus grew louder, Homer jumped up from his table, threw his napkin down, and told his son, "Come on, let's get in on the fun!" Homer had obviously had a flashback to his former life and was off and heading to the fight zone. Homer, Jr. grabbed his dad from behind and steered him back to their table. He held his dad by his shoulders until sound logic returned to the older man. Although he was now essentially a man of peace, he obviously clung to Teddy Roosevelt's doctrine of "speak softly and carry a big stick."

When Homer was teaching Scotty how to drive, he took him out on a seldom traveled rural road where his son could learn the basics of driving without having to dodge other cars. The lesson was going really well until Scotty hit a deep, bone-jarring pothole. Homer calmly told his son to stop the car. The confused Scotty did as he was told and looked to his dad for his next instructions. Homer then told Scotty to back the car up about fifty yards and stop. Once he had done so, Homer then told his son to drive forward and to hit a specific pothole up on the left side of the road. Scotty then asked his dad why he wanted him to hit that pothole. Homer glared at his son and replied, "Because that's the only damn pothole you've missed since you've been driving." Message delivered and message received. There was a limit to his dad's patience, and Scotty had exceeded it.

By the time he was a senior in high school, Homer, Jr. had wrecked several cars, some of them more than once. Homer had repeatedly lectured his oldest son about paying attention to his driving when he was behind the wheel. The older Homer, Jr. got, the more intense his dad's lectures had become. Homer Jr. had proven himself easily distracted throughout his school years. It was common for his teachers to write on his report cards, "Homer is easily distracted and spends far too much time staring out the window and daydreaming."

One night in October of his senior year, Homer, Jr. ran off the street, jumped the curb, and crashed into a sycamore tree in the

Spelling's front yard. When the police showed up, Homer, Jr. completed all of the paper work and then asked the policeman for a ride to Highway 80, where he could be dropped off. When the policeman asked him what his plans were after he reached Highway 80, the sorrowful and frightened high schooler told the policeman he was going to hitchhike to Dallas where he could join the Navy. The policeman put Homer in the back of the car, went into the Spelling's house and called the potential runaway's dad. He explained the situation to the older Homer and asked him what he wanted him to do with his son. Homer told him to please bring his son home.

When the officer came to the front door of the Eubanks home with Homer, Jr. in tow, Homer thanked the officer and escorted his son into their home. Homer did not tear into his son. Instead he simply told him to try harder and to always remember that home always represented the best refuge from just about any kind of storm.

Homer didn't cotton to overt stupidity like hitting potholes and ruining tires. However, the same man could flip the switch and rescue his sons from any trouble they were in or thought they were in. The boys always knew their dad was in their corner.

Even Homer's looks were a bit of a paradox. As a child, he had never seen a dentist so, as he grew up, his teeth gave him lots of problems, both health-wise and looks-wise. When he was in his forties, he replaced all of his teeth with false teeth. Wearing his new teeth improved his looks noticeably. To some people, he now looked a bit like a hardened version of Gary Cooper, who happened to be Homer's favorite actor. At bedtime, Homer put his new teeth in a glass in the bathroom and came out looking like Popeye. His boys started calling him Popeye and he just laughingly told them to check back in the morning and they would see Gary Cooper.

To his sons, Homer had lived his life darting back and forth across that invisible line of normality and convention. His actions really had often been paradoxical. He remained a puzzle his boys never completely solved, but they never lost their fascination with the man who was their father.

## Homer's End Times

By the start of the decade of the 1960s, Homer and Zee had helped their two oldest sons, Homer, Jr. and Robert, through college. Homer, Jr. had married his college sweetheart, Freddie Jordan in 1955, and Robert had moved to New Orleans, where he became a high school biology teacher and lived on Bourbon Street. He later married another teacher, Crystal Seeber. Having two sons out of the house and self-supporting gave Homer and Zelma a bit of financial freedom for the first time in a long time. Their youngest son, Scotty, had started high school and worked enough to be relatively self-sufficient. Zelma had a good job as Manager of the Boys Department at Sears, Homer's insurance business was doing well and both of their older boys were making it on their own. Homer, Jr. was, in fact, working with his dad in the insurance business.

In the glow of this new-found financial freedom, Homer and Zelma sold their 900 square foot home on Grove Street and bought a 1,600 square foot home on Marshall's upscale Merritt Street. The new house was much newer and featured three bedrooms as opposed to two; two bathrooms as opposed to one; showers as opposed to no showers; living room and a den as opposed to just a living room; and a built-in range as opposed to a rather small and antiquated stove. Central heating and air conditioning were the cherries on top of the ice cream.

The brick house sat on two well-manicured lots and featured a double garage and a small laundry room for a washer and dryer, items Zee had never enjoyed. Up until then, she had done their laundry at the laundromat–then referred to as the washateria in East Texas–located on South Washington Street. To Homer's delight, there was even a nice-sized work shed in the backyard, which Scotty quickly converted into a backyard get-away bedroom. It had electricity, an overhead fan and light, and a window. He added a rollaway bed and a small table. It never replaced his bedroom in the main house, but it was available for emergencies.

Homer brought four or five of his prized camellia plants from the old house and transplanted them on Merritt Street. He loved having a nice, new, large yard to "piddle" in and spent most of his spare time doing just that. He passed the mowing and raking jobs on to Scotty but retained the pruning, trimming, and manicuring for himself. Homer and Zee completely refurnished their new house, with the most expensive items going into their new formal living room. Homer made it well-known to his boys that the living room was reserved for special occasions and guests, and he laid out a few rules regarding the room's use. Some of the rules were: no eating or drinking in there, no napping on the new sofa, no use of the living room if you were sweaty or dirty, and no leaving items such as books, clothes, or sports equipment in the living room. Once the room had been completely furnished and accessorized, all that was left to do was to find something to hang over the sofa. Zee took charge of this chore and soon found a piece of "art" in the S&H Green Stamp catalogue she believed was perfect for that special spot.

Zee and Scotty spent the next few hours frantically gluing green stamps in their books. When all loose stamps had been glued in, Zee counted the number of books she had and proudly announced there were enough for the picture. Next, Homer, Zee, and Scotty drove straight to the S&H Green Stamp redemption center and traded their stamps for their new "art." It was a bucolic scene of a peaceful pond with lily pads scattered about and a huge weeping willow tree tilted out over the pond's edge. The white wood frame was perfect. Once it had been hung in its place of honor, Zee, Homer, and Scotty stepped back and stared lovingly at it for some time. In spite of its questionable provenance, the print was the Eubanks' first venture into the art world.

Scotty knew the new home and new furniture had to have put some economic pressure on his parents, as he was the one who delivered the payments to the savings and loan for the house and to McWilliams Furniture for their new furniture. The house payment was $94 a month and the furniture payment was $31 per month.

Homer was immensely proud of his new home, and he and Zee quickly established it as the gathering place for their family and friends. The three sons were thrilled watching their parents getting to enjoy a taste of economic success for the first time in a long time. Scotty now felt marginally wealthy, and everyone enjoyed watching Homer and Zee in their backyard playing with their first grandchild, Homer III. He had been born September 24, 1956. Buying the new house was a big thing to the entire family and served as a symbolic reward, of sorts, for Homer for having climbed the seemingly unclimbable hill that had financially and socially separated him from success. The sharecropper's son from Peno Bottom, Oklahoma, with the eighth-grade education had bucked the odds and climbed into the middle class.

In March of 1962, the old character actor, Walter Brennan, recorded a hit song entitled "Old Rivers," which was written by Cliff Clifford. In it, he talked the record instead of singing it, and his distinctive and rural voice was perfect for the nature of the song.

The story documented a young boy's friendship with an old, hardworking dirt farmer called Old Rivers; the boy talked about remembering his walking along behind the old man as he plowed his stingy soil behind his aged and decrepit mule named Midnight. He busted up dirt clods with his own bare feet as he trailed his friend Old Rivers. The boy told of how his friend, who was as poor as a church-mouse, would halt the plowing when the sun was at its hottest, lean back on the reins, and talk about a place he was gonna go.

Old Rivers would look off into the distance as he wiped the sweat from his brow and say, "…One of these days, I'm gonna climb up that mountain, walk up there among the clouds where the cotton's high and the corn's a-growin'…and there ain't no fields to plow…"

Homer, Jr., Robert, and Scotty quickly adopted that song as their dad's theme song. To them, Homer could have been the boy following his Papa in the field, or he could have been Old Rivers having to plow his way out of poverty. They weren't so eager to slot their dad into the song as they were to embrace the times, hardship, and loyalties of the period in history when their dad had been raised. The song just felt right for their dad. Robert latched onto the Old Rivers/dad connection and called him "Old Rivers" from that point on. Even letters to Homer and Zee from Louisiana were addressed to Mr. and Mrs. Old Rivers Eubanks. If Homer was irritated by his sons' teasing him and calling him "Old Rivers," he never acknowledged it. He would just chuckle and go on with his teaching of them.

The rapport between Homer and his boys stayed as strong as ever in the face of the two older boys leaving home and starting their own families. Homer was immensely proud of his two older boys getting their college degrees, and he found comfort in believing Scotty would get his as well.

This rally of good things for Homer continued in December of 1962, when Homer, Jr. and Freddie became parents of the first little girl in the Eubanks Family in two generations. Stephanie Jordan Eubanks was born December 29. Homer, who had often said the Eubanks Family was doing just fine with boys only, melted like ice cream in August when he first laid eyes on his new granddaughter. After Freddie and Stephanie went home from the hospital, Homer became quite adept at finding excuses to drop by for visits. Stephanie brought out the softer side of Homer, a side his boys had seldom seen. He would scoop her up and walk throughout the house and yard having private conversations with his new granddaughter. The last snapshot ever taken of Homer was one of him holding Stephanie three weeks before his death.

Some say little things that occur before the death of a loved one or other tragedies are revealed to have been omens of the bad event, especially when analyzed after the tragedy occurred. Two events took place just before Homer's sudden death that made

Scotty think there may be something to that assertion.

The first of those "omens" happened when Zelma came down with the flu two weeks prior to Homer's death. To play it safe, Homer moved into the twin bed next to Scotty's in his bedroom. For a full week, Homer and his youngest son discussed history, James Michener books, and life in general before they turned out the lights for the evening. It had been the first time the two had ever shared a bedroom and so many uninterrupted discussions. At the end of the week, the father and son were, perhaps, closer than they had ever been. Scotty felt that after their week together, he knew his dad better than he ever had before.

The second of those omens occurred the Monday morning before Homer's death on Tuesday, March 5, 1963. For some reason, Scotty was running late for school that morning and knew he would have to park a long way from campus if he drove himself to school, making him late for first period. Unexpectedly, Homer spoke up and told his son he would drop him off at school if he would kick it in gear. It was rare, indeed, for Homer to take his son to school.

Marshall High School was located on a hill, so when Homer pulled up to the campus' south edge, Scotty would have to run up the hill to school and Homer would drive downhill to return home. When Homer stopped the car to let Scotty jump out, he, uncharacteristically, leaned toward his son and offered his cheek for a good-bye peck. The surprised boy kissed his dad on the cheek and patted him three times–meaning I love you-on the shoulder. When Scotty got to the top of the hill, he turned to watch his dad drive away. His dad must have been watching his rearview mirror, because, without looking behind him, he waved three fingers to his son. His car then disappeared from Scotty's sight. Innately knowing this had been an odd, but special, good-bye, Scotty stood frozen in thought for a few minutes prior to entering his school. It was the last time he and his dad would exchange "I love yous."

## Marshall, Texas
## March 7, 1963

The funeral for Homer Alvin Eubanks, Sr, aged 54, was set for 2 p.m., Thursday, March 7, 1963. The two days prior to the service had been filled with making arrangements, finding accommodations for family members from out-of-town, receiving condolences from friends and neighbors, and trying to keep a stiff upper lip while fending off the urge and need to mourn. During those two days, the family spent more time entertaining their well-wishers than they did mourning and helping each other through that painful time. Flowers filled the living room of which Homer was so proud, and foods of all kinds filled the kitchen and dining area. Aunt Bon spent much of her time consoling Scotty and allowing him to vent his anger at God for taking his dad. Scotty and Bon wondered together whether Homer's and Zee's purchase of their new house had been heavenly inspired so Homer could be given a "first class" send-off.

In the evening, Zee, Homer, Jr., Robert, and Scotty, made time to discuss Homer's death. Zee primarily listened and nodded her approval as the boys dissected Homer as a father. They laughed as they retold his humorous stories, and they became very thoughtful as they reminded themselves of the many lessons of life he had taught them. Their dad had been their Oz; their "go to" guy who would always steer them in the right direction and seemed to know the answer to any question they could pose. The difference between Oz and Homer was that when the sons ripped away the curtain of awe that shielded him, it did not reveal a stumpy little mortal who had fooled everyone; it revealed a hero in every sense of the word. Their dad, Homer, had been the real thing.

Homer's story begs the question, "What is a hero?" Most would answer it is someone who performs heroic deeds for the good of others. The dictionary says it is "one of exceptional quality who wins admiration by noble deeds, especially deeds of courage." When his three sons closely examined the lofty status they had afforded their dad, they agreed without dissent that he was a true hero. They overlooked his occasional flings with his evil temptress lady alcohol, and they refused to declare her as his hamartia. To them, he had no fatal flaws that led to his downfall. He sometimes stumbled, but never fell down. They reasoned that anyone who gave you love, lived his life for your betterment, and consistently taught you how to get through life fairly and respectful of others, was a hero. Most people have their own heroes. Pity those who don't.

Did Homer deserve to have his biography written? He had not been a historic figure, a sports hero, a great general, or a noteworthy leader of the masses. He had only been a hero to three sons. Scholars believe that next to Jesus Christ, Abraham Lincoln has been biographized and written about more than any other person. They add that more than 15,000 books have been written about Honest Abe. He deserved it. There will never be other books written about Homer Eubanks–just this one. It is, however, the most important biography ever written to the Eubanks family.

A chapter ago, it was written that Walter Brennan's recording of the song, "Old Rivers" reminded the three Eubanks boys so much of their dad and the times and hardships of his growing up on a sharecropping farm that they began jokingly calling him Old Rivers. In the song, the young boy, who is now a man, has received a letter from home telling him that his friend, Old Rivers, has died. The news causes the boy to stare out across the field he was plowing and call to mind the countless times he had trailed behind that mule and Old Rivers busting up clods and looking for a bit of shade. As harsh as they were, the memories were good, and he leaned on his memories of Old Rivers saying, "one of these days I'm gonna climb that mountain, walk among the clouds where the cotton's high…and there ain't no fields to plow…"

Homer had no more fields to plow, and he left his three boys with many, many good memories to lean on. I was only sixteen at the time of his death, but I realize now that the sorrow I felt in 1963 was largely for my personal loss. However, the passage of time has given me a broader perspective. I now realize Homer had actually achieved his death. He had lived his life heroically and met all of the challenges life had laid at this feet and, although he lived only 54 years, he packed a lot of living into his life, and he packed a lot of life into his living.

*"I got a letter today from the folks back home and*
*they're all fine and crops is dry*
*down at the end my mama said, Son*
*you know Old Rivers died.*

*Just sittin' here now on this new-plowed earth*
*trying to find me a little shade*
*with the sun beatin' down 'cross the field I see*
*that mule, Old Rivers, and me.*

*Now one of these days*
*I'm gonna climb that mountain*
*walk up there among the clouds*
*where the cotton's high*
*and the corn's a-growin*
*and there ain't no fields to plow*
*with the sun beating down 'cross the field I see*
*that mule, Old Rivers, and me..."*

**Homer Eubanks, 1962**

## Epilogue

A family tightly bound by love usually marches through life as a cohesive unit. It usually pushes aside any thoughts of what life would be like when one or more of its members dies. Every family member knows it will happen, but not knowing exactly when it will happen enables the members to hope and pray it will happen sometime far in the future. In truth, it doesn't always work that way.

When Homer died at age 54, the family he left behind struggled for a while to regain its balance. Each family member latched onto the strength and independence with which Homer had imbued them.

Zelma, or Zee, became a widow at age 49. Though still a beautiful woman, she never re-married–or even dated–after Homer's death. She continued to work and continued to raise her 16-year-old son, Scotty. Zelma worked until she was well into her 70s. At age 79, she was diagnosed with Alzheimer's and died from the heartless disease at age 87.

Homer, Jr., the oldest of Homer and Zelma's three boys stepped up immediately after his dad's death and helped Zee replace his dad by taking care of the yard, automobiles, household repairs, and finance. He also, with brother Robert's help, provided the much younger Scotty with strong male leadership and understanding. Homer Jr. went to LSU on a football scholarship but a severe kidney injury he suffered his freshman year ended his gridiron career. After graduating from East Texas Baptist University, Homer, Jr. spent the majority of his professional life in credit union management. He and Freddie had a son, Homer III, and a daughter, Stephanie. Homer Jr. died of a heart attack at age 70. He was living in Lufkin, Texas at that time.

Robert, the middle son, lived in New Orleans and Baton

Rouge all of his post-college years. He stayed active in Scotty's academic endeavors throughout his remaining high school years and his four years in college. He also helped Scotty with school expenses. Robert had graduated from Stephen F. Austin State University and spent the majority of his professional life in pharmaceutical sales management. After retiring, he founded a new company that rented specialty hospital beds throughout Southern Louisiana. He and his wife, Crystal, had a son, Robert, Jr., and a daughter, Holly. Robert died of cancer at age 71 while living in Baton Rouge.

Scott Eubanks, who was 16 at the time of Homer's death, graduated from Stephen F. Austin State University in 1968 with a degree in Journalism/English. After college, he began a thirty-year career in economic development. During that time he headed the economic development programs for Oklahoma, Rhode Island, Virginia, and Arizona. Today, Scott and his son, Paul Scott, Jr., co-own an art gallery in Scottsdale, Arizona. He and wife Kay also have a daughter, Mary, who lives in Austin with her family. Scott has authored three books, all of which recount different facets of life within the Eubanks family.

www.ingramcontent.com/pod-product-compliance
Lightning Source LLC
Chambersburg PA
CBHW030443090526
44586CB00044B/666